101 QUESTIONS

ABOUT YOUR IMMUNE SYSTEM YOU FELT DEFENSELESS TO ANSWER . . . UNTIL NOW

101

QUESTIONS ABOUT YOUR

IMMUNE SYSTEM

YOU FELT DEFENSELESS TO ANSWER . . . UNTIL NOW

FAITH HICKMAN BRYNIE

Twenty-First Century Books

BROOKFIELD, CONNECTICUT

Published by Twenty-First Century Books
A Division of The Millbrook Press, Inc.
2 Old New Milford Road
Brookfield, CT 06804
www.millbrookpress.com

Library of Congress Cataloging-in-Publication Data
Brynie, Faith Hickman, 1946-
101 questions about your immune system you felt defenseless to answer . . .
until now / Faith Hickman Brynie.
    p.   cm.
Includes bibliographical references and index.
Summary: Questions and answers explain the human immune system and
how it works, as well as allergies and vaccines.
ISBN 0-7613-1569-1 (lib.bdg)
1. Immune system Juvenile literature.   2. Immunity Juvenile literature.
3. Allergy Juvenile literature.   4. Vaccines Juvenile literature.   [1. Immune
system Miscellanea.   2. Allergy Miscellanea.   3. Vaccines Miscellanea.
4. Questions and answers.]   I. Title.   II. Title: One hundred and one
questions about your immune system . . .   III. Title: One hundred one
questions about your immune system . . .
QR181.8.B79 2000   616.07'9-dc21   99-33368   CIP   AC

Cover photograph courtesy of NIBSC/SPL/Photo Researchers, Inc.

Photographs courtesy of © 1995 Peg Gerrity/Custom Medical Stock Photo:
p. 14; Visuals Unlimited: pp. 21 (top © Science VU/B. Ingelheim), 39 (© M.
Abbey), 67 (left © David M. Phillips, right © A. M. Siegelman), 69 (left ©
G. Shih-R. Kessel), 94 (left © R. Kessel-G. Shih, right © M. F. Brown), 132
(© K. G. Murti); Science Photo Library/Photo Researchers, Inc.: pp. 21
(middle Quest), 27 (CNRI), 69 (right © Dickson Despommier), 118 (©
Hank Morgan); Peter Arnold, Inc.: pp. 21 (bottom © David Scharf), 89 (©
John R. MacGregor); Purdue Photo/Dave Umberger: p. 29; Corbis/
Bettmann-UPI: p. 34; Joshua C. Goldstein: p. 44; Dr. Nikola Pavletich: p.
45; Lawrence DiFiori: p. 52; Reprinted from *Mayo Clinic Health Letter*
with permission of Mayo Foundation for Medical Education and Research,
Rochester, MN 55905: pp. 111, 114; Corbis/Jack Moebes: p. 127; Nicola
Kountoupes/Cornell University Photo: p. 130; Liaison Agency: p. 140 (©
Michael Schwarz); UNAIDS: p. 142; Dana-Farber: p. 146

CONTENTS

ACKNOWLEDGMENTS

The author wishes to thank the following experts for their insightful critical reviews: Dr. Carol Wyatt, Assistant Professor, Department of Veterinary Microbiology and Pathology, College of Veterinary Medicine, Washington State University; Dr. Paris Taylor Mansmann, Chair of the Basic and Clinical Immunology Committee of the American College of Allergy, Asthma, and Immunology, and Associate Professor of Medicine and Pediatrics at West Virginia University School of Medicine; and Dr. John Ninnemann, Dean of the College of the Sciences at Central Washington University. This book could not have been written without them.

Thanks also to Jason Henrie of the University of California, Davis, for his assistance with all things botanical; and to Cathrine Monson for her help with Four Corners geography.

The author also expresses gratitude to the following teachers and their students for their help in formulating the questions answered in this book: Mary Jane Davis, Red Bank Catholic High School, Red Bank, NJ; Tim Culp, Arroyo Grande High School, Arroyo Grande, CA; Jill Losee-Hoehlein, Great Bridge High School, Chesapeake, VA; and Mark Stephansky, Whitman-Hanson Regional High School, Whitman, MA. Thanks also to Kathy Frame of the National Association of Biology Teachers for making their involvement possible.

And, as always, thanks to Amy Shields, Senior Editor at Millbrook, who set this series within sight and within reach.

FOREWORD

Where the telescope ends, the microscope begins.
Which of the two has the grander view?
• VICTOR HUGO •

Like an astronomer probing the heavens in search of distant galaxies, biologists turn an eager eye inward—toward the miraculous universe of the living cell. There they find countless mysteries that intrigue and amaze. Powerful microscopes expand their vision. They use probes made not of metal but of molecules. Their laboratory? Not the expanses of space but the confines of a test tube.

Wherever their quest takes them, scientists find balance. Just as planets revolve in a stable orbit, living things maintain equilibrium. Life is balance: stability in times of change and renewal in times of calamity. Injury and illness threaten the finely tuned balance of human health. The immune system preserves balance. It prevents sickness when it can, and cures it when prevention fails. Some parts of the immune system react immediately against any threat, like the guard who shoots first and asks for a password later. Other parts are more cautious, identifying and assessing the threat before designing weapons of war. Either way, the goal is achieved. Balance returns. Life continues.

As you read and think about your immune system, you must think small. In this book you will gaze not into the vastness of quasars and black holes but into spaces beyond your closest vision. You'll be looking at models made to represent molecules too minute for the most powerful microscope to probe. Scientists guess how they are built from how they behave and use computers to draw their pictures. The microscope will show you viruses and bacteria powerful enough to defeat the strongest of men and women. These villains are so small that millions of them may be lurking even now on the period at the end of this sentence.

You may encounter some unfamiliar words in this book. For example, you'll read about enzymes in cells. What are enzymes? How do they work? Enzymes are protein molecules. They make chemical reactions happen, or they can stop reactions from happening, but they aren't part of the reaction. The reaction doesn't change them. Enzymes in and of themselves may not mean much to you, but if you keep the themes of change and balance in mind, you can create mental pictures so the words make better sense and their meanings stay with you longer.

For example, you might think of chemical reactions as the coupling and uncoupling of railway cars. Bouncing around unfettered in a railway yard, drifting and colliding at random, the cars might eventually hook together or unhook, but it could take a very long time for either to happen by chance. But what if a crew of railway workers were to arrive on the scene? They would quickly hook the cars together or take them apart as needed. When their job was done, they would take a break and wait until more cars came in. That's how enzymes work, and—just as a railroad couldn't run without workers—life would soon end without enzymes. They make sure that the right molecules join and break apart inside a cell.

In this book the elements of the immune system are often compared not to railroads but to armies. The nation under attack is the body. Enemy forces are tiny microbes that cause disease. The defending troops are the organs, tissues, and cells of the immune system. Macrophages and certain T cells are the infantry. They fight in close combat and gobble up invaders. The generals are certain kinds of T cells that command the action. B cells manufacture weapons. The bullets are proteins such as antibodies that lock onto disease-causing organisms. The toxic chemical weapons are enzymes—for example, those in the series called the complement system that dissolve and digest pathogens.

So complex is this war against illness that you need a roster to keep track of all the soldiers and their armaments. That's what Tables 1 through 3 in the back of the book are for. Can't remember the difference between B cells and T cells? Check Table 2. When you forget what interleukin is, Table 3 can help. There's also a glossary to refresh your memory if you forget a definition.

Those tools are here to help you, but don't worry too much about getting the exact term or chemical name right every time. Concentrate instead on the overall picture of how your immune system works. With appreciation and a sense of wonder, look inward at the dazzling expanses of life in balance. That universe is your immune system, and your study of it is a voyage beyond the stars.

CHAPTER ONE

20

QUESTIONS

THAT SHOULD
COME FIRST

When we die, microbes eat our bodies away.
When we are alive, microbes are trying to eat
our bodies. It is our immune system that protects us.

• PATRICK SCHLIEVERT •

**What Is
Immunity?**

Immunity is the ability to fight disease. Your body recognizes, attacks, and destroys foreign invaders—such as disease-causing viruses and bacteria—before they can do harm. Not all threats come from the outside. Sometimes, disease strikes from within, as when cancer cells multiply and form life-threatening tumors. Wherever the danger originates, the body has ways to fight back. That's immunity.

If all this sounds like armies on a battlefield, you have the idea. The invaders are pathogens (disease-causing microbes). The soldiers are white blood cells (leukocytes). The weapons are chemical. You would need a microscope to see this armed conflict, but its scale is as grand as any full-scale, human war.

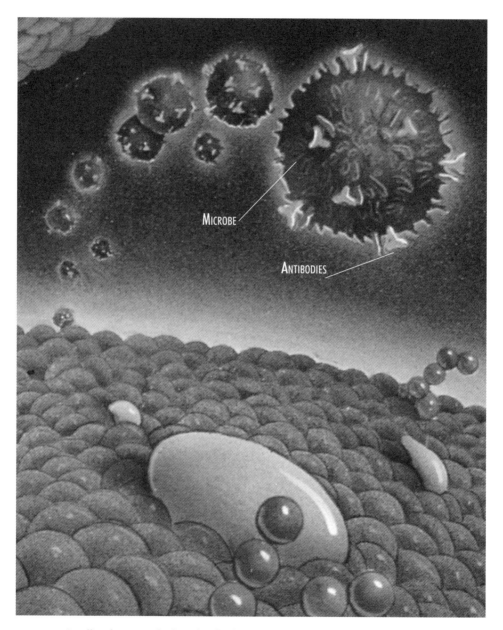

MICROBE

ANTIBODIES

B cells release antibodies that latch onto and destroy an invading microbe.

On this battlefield, protein molecules called antibodies latch onto microbes. They mark them for destruction or push them from the battlefield. Nearby, enzymes called complement dissolve and digest invaders. Several kinds of leukocytes are "eating cells." They gobble pathogens whole. Leukocytes called T cells often act as generals. They order B cells to produce and deploy antibodies. Throughout the engagement, the soldiers communicate using not radios but chemical messengers called cytokines, some of which do double duty as powerful weapons themselves.

If your health is good, your body's militia successfully attacks and destroys (or at least disarms) thousands of foreign invaders or potentially cancerous cells every day. When you feel well, you aren't aware of the conflict. When you feel ill, the immune system is losing the battle. Maybe the attacking force is too strong or its numbers are too great for your immune system to prevail right away. But no war is won or lost in a single battle. Most of the time, the immune system wins in the long run. You get well and feel better, ready to fight the next war with some unknown enemy.

How Does My Body Prevent Microbes From Invading?

Your skin is your first line of defense. It serves as a nearly impenetrable protection against most microbes. But the skin is much more than a passive barrier like a film of plastic wrap. It can disarm invaders and detoxify many poisons, too.

Several different kinds of skin cells get into the act. For example, Langerhans cells in the skin's outermost layer ingest microbes. Then they attach some of the microbe's proteins to their surfaces. When T cells detect foreign proteins, they order the manufacture of antibodies. Antibodies patrol like palace guards. They grab foreign proteins and stop them in their tracks. You'll find them at work in sebum, the oily

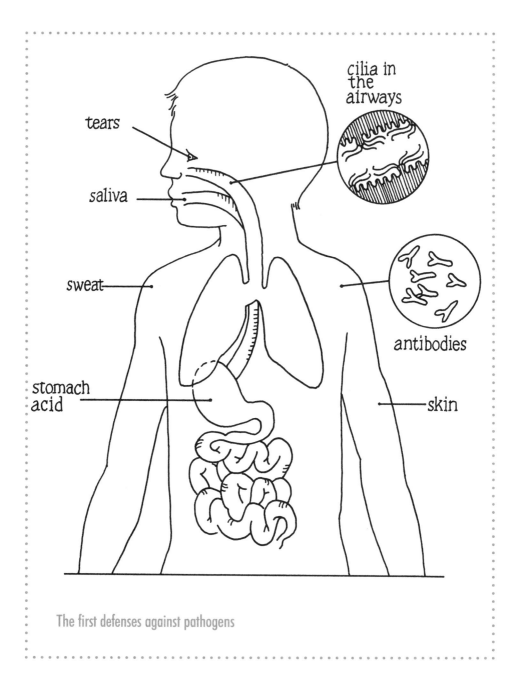

cilia in
the
airways

tears

saliva

sweat

antibodies

stomach
acid

skin

The first defenses against pathogens

substance that keeps hair shiny and skin supple. They also turn up in sweat, tears, saliva, and mucus.

Pathogens can enter the body through its natural openings, such as the nose and mouth. Tonsils and adenoids at the back of the throat and nose block invaders of both the airways and digestive system. In the breathing passages, cilia are tiny hairlike structures that sway like grass in the wind. They project from cells that line the nose and airways. They snag dirt, dust, and microbes and expel them from the body. Sneezes, coughs, and runny noses discharge microbial invaders. Chemical weapons are often used. The hydrochloric acid of the stomach kills most, if not all, of the bacteria that enter in food and water. Enzymes in tears and saliva dissolve microbes in the eyes and mouth.

How Does My Body Fight Pathogens That Get Past Its Outer Defenses?

Immune cells move through the body in blood and lymph. Blood has a closed circulation. It stays inside the blood vessels. Lymph is the clear fluid that bathes every cell in the body. It moves outside the blood, carrying many different types of immune cells, including phagocytes (their name means "eating cells") that gobble invaders. Lymph circulates through a series of interconnected vessels, but the system lacks the pumping action that propels blood from the heart to the rest of the body. Lymph moves by gravity and muscle action. The cells that circulate in lymph make their way back to the bloodstream eventually.

Lymph nodes are nodules in the neck, groin, chest, abdomen, and armpits. Along with the spleen, they act as filters, trapping disease-causing organisms and removing them from circulation. The lymphatic tissues that line the intestine are the largest part of the immune system. Included here are Peyer's patches, lymph nodes at the end of the small intestine.

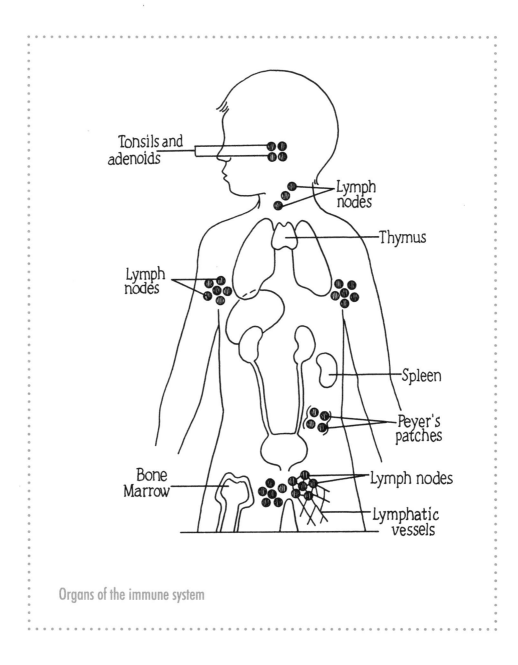

Tonsils and adenoids

Lymph nodes

Thymus

Lymph nodes

Spleen

Peyer's patches

Bone Marrow

Lymph nodes

Lymphatic vessels

Organs of the immune system

The 15 or 20 enzymes of the complement system work in both blood and lymph.[1] Complement produces a series of chemical reactions, each dependent upon the one before it. Any number of proteins, antibodies, or sugars from the cell walls of bacteria can start the sequence rolling, like dominoes falling in a line across a gymnasium floor. Once the chain reaction begins, complement enzymes (1) release chemicals that recruit immune cells to the site; (2) attach a protein "marker" or "flag" to an invader cell, which attracts phagocytes; or (3) destroy a microbe by poking holes in its membrane. Complement doesn't know friend from foe. It wipes out all in its path. That's why complement requires inactivators to stop it once started.

What Cells Make Up My Immune System?

The cells of the immune system, like soldiers in an army, bear names that identify their type, rank, and mission. All are leukocytes, but each has a different structure and a different job.

First are the lymphocytes. They are made in the bone marrow, liver, and spleen and set loose into the bloodstream. In every organ except the brain, they diffuse out of the blood vessels and move among the tissues, "searching" for microbes and foreign proteins. Eventually they return to the blood with the lymph. T cells are one kind of lymphocyte. They mature and develop in the thymus gland, which lies just behind the breast bone.

Three types of T cells are important defenders:

- Helper T cells, also called CD4 cells, signal the B cells to start producing antibodies or to speed up production.
- Suppressor T cells slow or stop the manufacture of antibodies, although how they achieve this is unknown.

- Killer T cells, also called cytotoxic T cells or CD8 cells, kill invaders by splitting their cell membranes with enzymes. They also destroy cancer cells and cells infected with viruses.

B cells are also lymphocytes. They arise and develop in bone marrow. They mature into plasma cells and become antibody factories. The human body normally contains more than 100 billion B cells.[2] Each can make a unique antibody molecule, different from that made by any other B cell.

Any wandering microbe that sneaks through the body's first defenses eventually runs into a phagocyte. Phagocytes capture and engulf microbes, digesting them with enzymes and absorbing their parts. Phagocytes do something many cells cannot; they can move into the brain.

Monocytes are the largest phagocytes. They move with the blood, consuming any foreign invaders they come across. Macrophages are similar to monocytes, but they don't circulate. They reside among the cells they serve. Their name means "big eater." They live up to their name by devouring any microbes that come their way.

Macrophages act as one kind of "antigen-presenting" cell. (An antigen is any particle or molecule that triggers an immune response.) After such cells consume an invader, they display some of its proteins on their outer membranes. T cells inspect membrane proteins regularly. When they spot a foreign protein, T cells give the order that starts B cells making antibodies. But not just any antibody. Each kind of antibody precisely matches the protein detected on the antigen-presenting cell.

Dendritic cells are also antigen-presenters. They capture antigens that travel to the spleen and lymph nodes and present them to T cells. Dendritic cells are often called the pacemakers of the immune system. They are important regulators of the antibody response.

Neutrophils, the most numerous leukocytes in the blood, belong to a class of cells called granulocytes. All granulocytes are made in

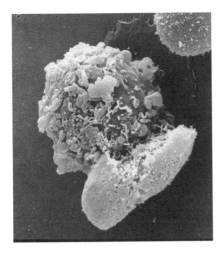

Left: The oval cell in the foreground is a cancer cell, disintegrating after being attacked by the round T-lymphocyte cell in background.

Right: An eosinophil cell. The smaller dark spots in the cell contain both enzymes which destroy bacteria, and rod-shaped crystals, the function of which is not known.

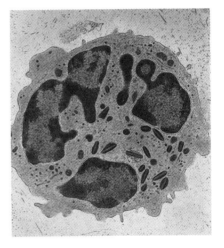

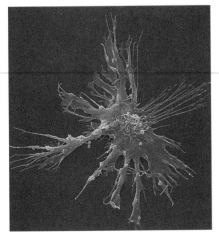

Left: A dendritic cell of the immune system

bone marrow. Their granules act as storage depots for infection-fighting chemicals. To release the chemical weapons, the granules fuse with the cell membrane. That opens the granule to the outside, and its contents spill out.

Basophils are also granulocytes. Their granules contain an agent that prevents blood from clotting. Yet a third type is the eosinophil, which clears large complexes of cells or molecules from the blood. High levels of eosinophils often indicate that the body is fighting a parasite such as a worm. Allergies can send eosinophil levels soaring, too.

Mast cells are yet another type of granulocyte. Both basophils and mast cells slow blood flow and make tissues leak fluid. Like eosinophils, mast cells play a part in allergies. Mast cells release histamine, a chemical that both kills invaders and irritates body cells. Histamine makes your nose run when you have a cold. It does the same to hay fever sufferers when the grass pollens fly.

Yet another kind of leukocyte has a special job to do. Natural killer, or NK, cells secrete an enzyme that dissolves the membranes of cells that display foreign or abnormal proteins. Along with killer T cells, NKs are powerful weapons against many cancer cells and cells infected with viruses.

Are Antibodies and Antibiotics the Same Thing? No. Antibodies are Y-shaped proteins made by B cells. They circulate in blood and latch onto invaders, tagging them for destruction. Antibiotics are chemicals that kill bacteria. They occur naturally in soil. Microbes make them. Scientists have found ways to turn them into medicines. So when your doctor prescribes antibiotics, your body is probably making antibodies already.

Ancient people realized that the body must have ways to fight disease. Nothing else could explain why having a disease once meant never having it again. Not until the late nineteenth and early twentieth centuries did attempts to explain the immune system begin. Investigators realized that the immune system must have ways to:

- classify: determine what is "self" and what is "not self."
- identify: distinguish one invader from another.
- switch on: respond when a pathogen invades.
- switch off: stop when danger passes.
- remember: store information about an enemy encountered in the past.

Today, we know that antigen molecules on the surfaces of cells are responsible for all five. Antigens are usually proteins, often bound to sugars that change their shape. Antigens may be formed in the body or enter from outside. Antigens on the surfaces of bacteria or viruses trigger an immune response. So do the pollen, dust, and animal dander that cause allergies in susceptible people. In that case, antigens are also allergens.

What are proteins? Protein molecules are chains of smaller molecules called amino acids. Twenty different kinds of amino acids make up human proteins. Amino acids are made of atoms of carbon, hydrogen, oxygen, nitrogen, and sometimes phosphorus and sulfur. There's nothing special about these atoms, but the arrangement of amino acids in proteins is special. Every kind of protein is different because of the number, order, and arrangement of its amino acids. The amino acid sequence determines the shape that a protein molecule will twist and fold into.

The shape of the protein is the key to antigen recognition. The immune system can tell one protein from another by its form—but only if the shape is exposed on a cell surface in a particular way.

The recognition of "self" versus "not self" depends on antigens on the surface of body cells. Cell membranes display MHC (major histocompatibility complex) proteins on their surfaces. MHC proteins act as docks. They tether antigens to cell surfaces so that the immune system can examine the shape. By shape, "self" and "not self" are recognized.

T cells, B cells, and plasma cells all play a part in the immune system's "memory." Your body does not make every possible kind of antibody all the time—only those that are needed at the moment. Once antibod-

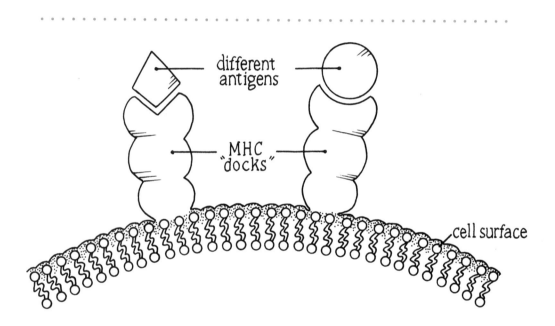

different antigens

MHC "docks"

cell surface

The shape of an antigen docked on a cell's surface cues the immune system to recognize it as "self" (belonging to the body) or "not self" (an invader from the outside). Antigens of both types can trigger an immune response.

ies have done their job, most disappear within a few weeks. But some of the cells that triggered antibody production survive. They travel to the lymph nodes where they become memory cells. The next time you encounter that same antigen, the memory cells trigger immediate and rapid antibody production.

Switching off the immune response is as important as switching it on. In all its functions, the body must maintain homeostasis—that is, balance. The soldiers must rally when attacked but must settle to a peaceful, resting state when the war is over. If they didn't, too many immune cells would overload the system and harm healthy tissue. Antibody production ceases because suppressor T cells give the order to shut down. The action of killer T cells must stop at some point, too. Chemicals produced by the T cells themselves inhibit the growth of more T cells. They trigger the death of most that remain, with the exception of the few that become memory cells.

How Do I Become Immune to a Disease?

Immunity can be:

- innate: You are born with it.
- acquired: You get it as a result of some interaction with your environment.
- shared: You aren't immune, but you enjoy the benefits of immunity because you are a member of a group in which most others are immune.

You were probably born with some immunities you don't know you have. Any time a disease strikes a large group of people, some individuals escape it. Maybe they are just lucky. Or maybe they were born with genetic information that confers immunity to a particular pathogen. Their cells may make a particular protein that destroys the microbe or prevents it from entering cells. Every person's genetic makeup is unique (except for identical twins), and some of those genetic differences confer innate immunity.

Acquired immunity comes not from inheritance but from the experiences of living. If you have chicken pox once, you won't get it again. That's because memory cells "remember" the chicken pox virus and attack it the instant it shows up again. You can acquire immunity by having a disease or getting a vaccine.

Scientists call the immunity that comes from membership in a group "herd immunity." Here's how it works. Imagine yourself back in the first grade. Everyone in your class gets the measles at about the same time. You are away from school that week, perhaps on a trip with your parents. When you return, your classmates have all recovered. They are immune to measles because they have had the disease. You're not. Still, you won't get measles because there's no one to catch the disease from. You can contract measles if you move into another class where the disease is spreading, but as long as you stay with your classmates, you won't get the measles. You are, in effect, immune because your "herd" is immune.

How Do Pathogens Make Me Sick? Many diseases—but by no means all—are caused by microbes. The word microbe is a general term meaning a living thing too small to see without a microscope. Bacteria and many fungi and protozoa fall into this category. Other disease-causers are so simple that they cannot truly be considered living. These are the viruses. Made of nothing more than a strand of genetic material (DNA or RNA) covered by a protein coat, viruses cannot reproduce on their own. They must inhabit a living cell.

Among the millions of different kinds of microbes and viruses, only a few are human pathogens. Some cause sickness directly; they kill the cells they infect. Others do their damage indirectly through the poisons or toxins they give off as waste products. Toxins can kill host cells or interfere with their function. Diphtheria, tetanus, and botulism are all toxin diseases.

Many viruses cause illness because they destroy cells. Viruses enter a cell and take over its "command and control" center—the DNA in the cell's nucleus. There they direct the cell to produce more viruses. The cell eventually bursts open and dies, releasing millions of viruses. The symptoms of viral diseases depend on the cells they invade. Influenza is a viral infection that settles in the breathing passages. AIDS is a viral infection of helper T cells.

These are two *Staphylococcus aureus* bacteria. The cell wall of the bacterium on the upper left has been destroyed by antibiotics, and you can see the cellular material leaking out.

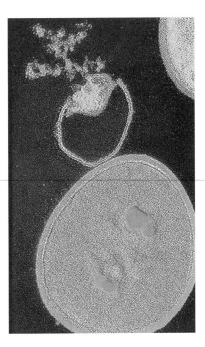

What Causes the Common Cold? Viruses cause colds. A cold virus infects the cells of your nose, throat, and airways long before you become aware of the symptoms: sneezing, coughing, runny or congested nose, watery eyes, fatigue, headache, aching muscles. Many of your cold symptoms come not from the virus but from the immune system's attempts to fight it. For example, virus-fighting chemicals irritate nasal passages and cause fluid to drip or gush. That gets rid of viruses, but the runny nose makes you uncomfortable.

Why Do I Get Colds Every Year, Year After Year? More than 200 known viruses cause colds. Some cause only minor respiratory infections in both children and adults. Others produce mild symptoms in adults but make children seriously ill. The number of cold-causing viruses is always growing.[3] That's because viruses are very good at mutating (changing their genetic material). The result? Children average some six to ten colds a year. Adults can expect two to four.[4]

Perhaps half or more of all colds are caused by a family of viruses called rhinovirus.[5] Michael Rossmann and Jordi Bella at Purdue University used X rays to probe crystals of Rhinovirus 16. Computer models showed some 60 places on its surface capable of attaching to human cells.[6] The virus hooks onto molecular anchors on cells that normally hold leukocytes in place at the sites of injuries. Ironically, the rhinoviruses have found a way to use one of the body's protective mechanisms as an entryway for infection.

Rhinovirus is actually a "family name" for many different kinds of cold-causing viruses. After you recover from a cold, you will be immune to the specific rhinovirus that infected you, but not to other members of the rhinovirus family. As you grow older, you gain more and more specific immunities. As a result, colds become rarer.

Purdue University researcher Jordi Bella views a computer model of the Rhinovirus 16 cold virus.

What Is Inflammation?

Inflammation is the swelling, redness, pain, heat, and stiffness you experience with any injury or irritation. It results from a chain of immune reactions. At the site of an injury, the area turns red and swells because the walls of the blood vessels get "leaky." They let fluid and immune cells escape from the bloodstream. Immune cells rush to the site in large numbers. Phagocytes gobble up microbes. Antibodies tag invaders for destruction by enzymes.

The first immune cells on the scene send chemical signals that attract more defensive cells to the area. As the war rages on, dead tissue and excess fluid litter the battlefield. Lymph washes some of the debris away. Phagocytes consume the rest. Dead and dying cells are carried to the lymph nodes for disposal. On the outside, this looks like red, swollen tissue. Although inflammation may cause you pain, it's actually a good sign. It lets you know that your immune system is fighting an invader.

How Do Antibodies Work?

Some antibodies tag invaders for consumption by phagocytes. Others activate the complement system. Still others block the entry of viruses into body cells.

Antibodies are Y-shaped proteins. They have molecular "hooks" on the arms of the Y that attach to a specific antigen. The antibody is like a key. It precisely fits the "lock" of the invading antigen. By fitting into an antigen—like a key in a lock—the antibody can mark the antigen for destruction.

B cells make antibodies, but they don't swing into production until helper T cells give the order. T cells don't give the order until they spot a foreign antigen. Antigen-presenting cells, such as macrophages, do what their name suggests. They chop invaders into pieces and display some of the invaders' proteins on their surfaces. When a helper T cell spots an antigen that's "not self," it sends the signal for B cells to make antibodies. Each antibody is specifically designed to match the shape of the invading antigen. Not just any B cell can do this. B cells that mature into plasma cells specialize in making antibodies.

Are All Antibodies the Same?

No. Each is unique. Just like a single key fits a single lock, each antibody binds a single antigen. Every invading antigen must be fought with a specific antibody. The body can make millions of different kinds—each especially suited to the antigen it must combat. The body doesn't waste energy making all possible antibodies all the time. It makes only what's needed, when needed.

How is this done? Plasma cells contain the genetic information (DNA) that directs them to make not whole antibodies but antibody pieces. Fitting those pieces together in different ways makes possible millions of different combinations. The strategy is much the same as using an alphabet to write a language. In English, a mere 26 letters can spell millions of different words. In the same way, a small number of genes can direct the production of antibodies in infinite variety.

Antibodies are also called immunoglobulins. Although each is unique, five general categories classify them (with the Ig standing for immuno-globulin in each case):

- IgG is a powerful and wide-ranging antibody found throughout the organs and blood vessels.
- IgA occurs mainly in fluids such as saliva, tears, breast milk, and digestive juices.
- IgM is so large it stays inside blood vessels.
- IgD occurs on the outer membranes of B cells. It helps identify foreign antigens.
- IgE locks onto mast cells and basophils and causes them to release histamine and other chemicals that fight large invaders such as parasites. Unfortunately, IgE too often responds to harmless allergens just as it would to a parasite. That produces the symptoms of allergies.

How Do the Parts of My Immune System Communicate?

Chemistry is the language of immunity. Proteins that influence immune function are called cytokines. Cytokines can attach to the membranes of some body cells and not others. That fact allows cytokines to carry messages between cells and tissues. A large number of cytokines have been found. Their names include interleukins, interferons, colony-stimulating factors, tumor necrosis factors, chemokines, growth factors, and more.

When cells infected with viruses die, they release interferons. Interferons induce healthy cells to manufacture an enzyme that kills viruses. Three types of interferon bear the names of letters of the Greek alphabet—alpha, beta, and gamma. Among many other functions, alpha and beta interferon stimulate the numbers and activity of killer T cells. Gamma interferon activates macrophages.

The interleukins do many jobs, too. Interleukin-1 activates lymphocytes and stimulates macrophages. Interleukin-2 spurs killer T cells into action. It incites them to destroy cells infected with virus or possibly cancerous cells. As many as 30 interleukins have been identified. Each performs more than one function and interacts with other cytokines in complex ways.

Other cytokines called colony-stimulating factors stimulate the growth and reproduction of particular cells. Growth factors help injured bones, skin, and nerves to heal. The cytokine called tumor necrosis factor kills cancer cells directly or shrinks tumors by cutting off their blood supply. Chemokines attract T cells, monocytes, and neutrophils to inflammatory sites.

Does My Immune System Attack Microbes or the Cells They Infect? That question provoked a lot of argument among scientists at the beginning of the twentieth century.

Two opposing camps formed: One group thought the immune system works because antibodies attach to invading antigens and mark them for destruction. That's called humoral immunity. (Humor means "fluid," and antibodies circulate in fluids: blood and lymph.) The other believed that leukocytes destroy infected cells—microbe, cell, and all. That's called cellular or cell-mediated immunity.

It turned out that both views are correct. The immune system deploys two separate, but cooperating, forces. The difference depends on the MHC (major histocompatibility complex) proteins of antigen-presenting cells. Scientists divide MHC proteins into two categories: class I and class II.

MHC class II proteins serve as "docking stations" on the surfaces of antigen-presenting cells such as macrophages. When a macrophage gobbles up an invading microbe, it docks antigens from the invader on its MHC class II port. Helper T cells check these docking ports regularly. When they detect an antigen that shouldn't be there, they signal the B cells to make antibodies.

Viruses have ways around this defense. They get inside cells and hide where antibodies can't get to them. That's where cell-mediated immunity comes in. On the cell's surface lie other docking ports, the MHC class I proteins. The cell ferries some of the viral antigens out of the interior and onto the MHC class I docks. Killer T cells look out for foreign proteins attached to MHC I sites. When a viral antigen appears there, killer T cells destroy the cell—and the virus along with it. MHC class I proteins also ferry fragments from cancer cells to the surface, where T cells can recognize them as abnormal. Once identified, enzymes that split the cell open and spill its contents destroy the entire cell. In summary:

Type of Immunity:	Humoral ("in the fluids")	Cell-mediated
Invader:	Any microbe or foreign protein (outside cell)	Virus (inside cell) or abnormal cancer cell
Cell type:	Specialized antigen-presenting cells engulf invader.	Any kind of cell
Docking port:	MHC class II	MHC class I
Outcome:	Helper T cells trigger antibody response.	Killer T cells destroy cancerous or virus-infected cell.
Mechanism:	Antibodies bind to antigens, which either (1) attract phagocytes; (2) activate complement; or (3) prevent viruses from entering cells.	Enzymes burst infected or cancerous cells open.

In 1971 a boy named David was born in Houston, Texas. At first, David seemed healthy, but soon his tragic condition was discovered. Born with abnormal stem cells in his bone marrow, David's body could manufacture neither T cells nor B cells. Even the slightest contact with a pathogen could kill David.

David, finally able to enjoy a hug from his mother, courtesy of his space suit from NASA.

In an attempt to save his life, his doctors placed him inside a sterile plastic enclosure. The bubble kept him away from all sources of infection. No dirty hands touched him. The bubble sterilized the air he breathed. David ate only sterilized food. As he grew, larger bubbles were built for him. NASA even constructed a "space suit" that let David move around. David became famous as "The Boy in the Bubble."

As David got older, his family and doctors realized that he could not grow into adulthood living in a bubble. Didn't David have a right to a family, a job, and a home of his own? The MHC antigens on David's sister's cells were similar—although not identical—to David's. If her stem cells could grow in David's bone marrow, he had a chance of manufacturing the T cells and B cells that could free him from his bubble,

At age twelve, David received a transplant of his sister's bone marrow. In the early days after the operation, all went well. The stem cells in David's transplanted bone marrow began to produce leukocytes. But along with stem cells, David had received a virus from his sister. The virus had no effect on her healthy immune system, but it proved fatal for David.

David's condition is called SCID—severe combined immunodeficiency disease. Most immune deficiencies are less severe than David's, but some can be equally life-threatening.

Can immune deficiency diseases be treated?

Yes, better now than in the 1970s. One child with an immune deficiency became almost as famous as David, but for a different reason. Ashanti DeSilva was born missing a gene that codes for an enzyme called ADA. T cells can't work without that enzyme, so Ashanti's health was poor.

In 1990, Ashanti, then a shy and charming four-year-old, made medical history. A team of doctors led by W. French Anderson received permission to try gene therapy with Ashanti. They took some T cells from her blood, exposed them to viruses carrying the normal gene (which Ashanti was missing), and then returned them to her blood. The doctors hoped that the virus would "infect" her blood cells with the normal gene. The therapy worked. Some of her blood cells began making the enzyme she was missing. Because

- -

How Ashanti's gene therapy worked.

Healthy gene is spliced into the genes of a virus engineered to be harmless. The virus then "infects" a white blood cell taken from the patient. The DNA from the healthy gene is passed along to the white blood cell with the DNA from the virus. The "new" white blood cells are injected back into the patient to multiply.

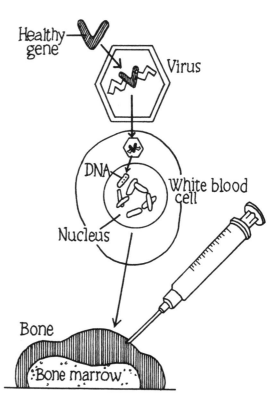

- -

the altered cells died off, Ashanti needed continuing treatment, but with each injection her T cell function improved.

Ashanti's condition is only one among some approximately 70 known inborn deficiencies of the immune system.[7] Immune deficiencies can also develop later in life. For example, viral infections, radiation, or toxins can bring on an acquired deficiency. One commonly used treatment for immune deficiencies is gamma globulin, the part of the blood that contains antibodies. About 100,000 people in the United States alone depend on regular injections of gamma globulin to survive.[8]

Will My Immune System Weaken or Grow Stronger as I Grow Older?

Your immune system will be at its strongest in young adulthood. As you get older, you will produce fewer T cells, which don't work quite as well as the ones your young body made. B cells get less efficient over time, too. They gradually become less adept at copying themselves and releasing antibodies. As you age, your antibodies also become increasingly likely to attack your own tissues, making autoimmune diseases most common among the elderly (see Chapter 5).

Remember the thymus, that small gland in your chest that "trains" T cells? It's largest in early childhood. It begins to shrink in the early teens and gets smaller as the years pass, disappearing completely in old age. The thymus continues to produce T cells into adulthood, but as it shrinks, its ability to produce T cells shrinks with it.

Are Human and Animal Immune Systems Alike?

Similar, but not identical.

It took a Russian, a starfish, and a rose thorn to uncover one basic similarity. In 1883, the Russian zoologist Élie Metchnikoff stayed home while his family went to the circus. More exciting for Metchnikoff than acrobats and elephants was observing starfish through his microscope. For years, he had been studying the digestive systems of their tiny larvae, in which ameba-like cells could ebb and flow, absorbing and digesting minute food particles from the sea.

> Metchnikoff wrote of that day:
> [A] new thought suddenly flashed across my brain.... It struck me that similar cells might serve in the defense of the organism against intruders.... If my supposition were true, a splinter introduced into the body of a starfish larva, devoid of blood vessels or of a nervous system, should soon be surrounded by mobile cells as is to be observed in a man who runs a splinter into his finger.[9]

To test his idea, Metchnikoff plucked a rose thorn from his garden and poked it into a starfish larva. By his own account, he was too excited to sleep that night, so eager was he for the results. He rushed to his microscope the next morning to find his suspicions confirmed. Around the thorn gathered a horde of cells eating away at the intruder.

Metchnikoff called the process phagocytosis, and the cells performing it, phagocytes. Phagocytes in various forms operate in all animals, whether simple or complex. Insects, starfish, frogs, sharks, and human beings all have phagocytes. All depend on them for their survival.

The similarities do not stop with phagocytes. Primitive animals can distinguish "self" from "not self." Graft a piece from one sponge to another, and the host will reject the transplant. But the graft will be rejected no more quickly the second time than the first. That means sponges lack the memory functions of higher animals.

Primitive animals even have a cytokine system of sorts. Researchers Gregory Beck and Gail Habicht found substances similar to interleukin-

1 and tumor necrosis factor in worms and sea squirts. Molecules much like interleukins 1 and 6 turn up in the tobacco hornworm.

Among animals more closely related to humans, the similarities become even greater. Sharks possess antigen-presenting molecules remarkably similar to the MHC molecules of humans and other mammals. They have spleens, just like people. Their spleens manufacture B cells and help clear the body of bacteria. Sharks make immunoglobulins, but only one, IgM, is the same as a human type.

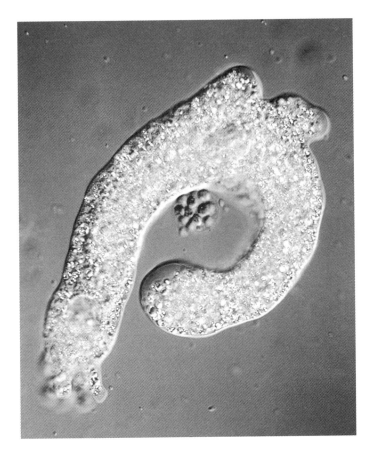

An amoeba in the midst of the phagocytosis process surrounds algae, the dark mass of dots, which it will digest.

Not the same as animals, but plants do have ways of fending off invaders. Plants may endure temperature changes from very cold at night to hot during the day, a range too great for most pathogens to tolerate. The same holds for humidity. Many plants can stand both wet and dry periods, something that foils many microbes. Some plants use chemical weapons from the soil. They accumulate heavy metals and store them in "packets" called vacuoles. When pathogens attack, the vacuoles burst and release the metals, which poison invaders.

Many plants produce chemical substances that either kill or repel microbes. One example is the saponins found in oats, potatoes, spinach, tomatoes, and other food plants. So effective are saponins in fighting infections in plants, some researchers think they offer promise as drugs for treating disease in humans.

Plants carry genes that provide them with natural resistance to many infections. For example, certain tomato plants make proteins that bind to antigens on an invading microorganism, preventing it from penetrating the plant. These proteins give the tomatoes a natural immunity to a disease called bacterial speck disease. Scientists in California and Indiana isolated a gene for this protein and transferred it to tobacco plants. Transplanting the gene transplanted immunity. Their tobacco plants can resist bacterial speck disease.

The most elegant of plant defense systems is called gene silencing. The plant "analyzes" the genetic material in a viral invader and manufactures a defensive protein that binds it—in much the same way as animals use antibodies. The silencing response isn't limited to infected cells. It spreads throughout the plant and concentrates in newly dividing cells at growth points. In this way, plant cells far from the site of the original infection are prepared to resist the virus. According to Washington State University biochemist James Carrington, "Immune systems that can recognize new viruses were thought to be a unique property of animals. Now we know that plants have a flexible, adaptive defense response that may be just as effective as the human immune system in limiting damage due to viruses."[10]

Suicide:
Can't Live Without It

- - - - -

Apoptosis . . . the ultimate act of biological altruism.
UNIDENTIFIED AUTHOR WRITING IN *THE ECONOMIST*

- - - - -

Have you seen the 1997 Academy Award winning movie *Titanic?* The end of this love story moves viewers to the edges of their seats, wondering if Jack Dawson (Leonardo DiCaprio) will die to save Rose Bukater (Kate Winslet).

The scene is riveting because self-sacrifice is the greatest of all possible acts of benevolence.

The cells of your body do it every day.

Cellular suicide or programmed cell death is called apoptosis (pronounced ah puh TOE sus). The name comes from a Greek word describing leaves falling from trees. Some cancer researchers coined the term in 1972, but no one paid much attention. Twenty years later, apoptosis boomed as "the hottest field of medical science."[11] "It's like the Theory of Relativity," said Gerard Evan of the Imperial Cancer Research Fund in London. "It changes the way you think about everything."[12]

Why did it take so long for scientists to recognize something so important? Probably because the notion that death sustains life took some getting used to. "Everybody thought about death as something you didn't want to happen," says Barbara Osborne of the University of Massachusetts. "Sometimes it takes a while for something to sink in."[13]

The first thing to sink in was that apoptosis is very different from necrosis, the death of cells due to injury, defect, or aging. Necrosis is a violent death. Many cells die. Their membranes burst, and their contents spill out. Deadly enzymes flood neighboring cells, causing inflammation and more cell death. In contrast, apoptosis is orderly and safe. Cells die one at a time. Enzymes inside the cell cut its membrane into neat pieces and store them for recycling. Apoptosis wastes no energy or raw materials. It releases no harmful enzymes.

You can watch the early stages of apoptosis through a microscope. The cell curls into a tight ball. Its membrane pulses, poking out knobs called blebs. Inside, enzymes called caspases dismantle the cell. Each caspase controls a single step in the process—from snipping DNA into measured pieces to bundling cell parts into membrane-bound packets. Once the packets are sealed, macrophages and neighboring cells ingest them.

What's the point of expending all this energy only to effect cellular suicide? At least once every day, your immune system destroys a cell that would become a cancer if it lived.[14] Some cancers result from virus infec-

tions. When a virus-infected cell commits suicide, the virus is disassembled and packaged right along with everything else in the cell. The virus no longer exists. It cannot cause cancer.

What triggers apoptosis? On the membrane of many cells lies a protein called Fas. T cells make a protein called FasL (for Fas ligand—ligand comes from a Latin word meaning "bind" or "tie"). The binding of FasL to Fas pushes the cell's "panic button." It initiates the self-destruct sequence. Cell suicide is swift—complete within an hour.[15]

Genes make sure that apoptosis occurs at the right time and place. A gene in the nucleus directs the cell to make a protein called p53. The p53 protein acts as a quality-control inspector. It checks the DNA of the cell. DNA, the master molecule in the nucleus, can be damaged, either by chance during division or by exposure to radiation or poison. The p53 protein searches out DNA defects. When damage is found, p53 sounds the alert. Repair enzymes swing into action and fix minor damage. Major damage may be beyond repair. In that case, p53 pushes the self-destruct button, and apoptosis begins. How p53 makes such a "decision" remains a mystery.

This remarkable sequence of time-lapse microscopy shows the death of two tumor cells after exposure to radiation.

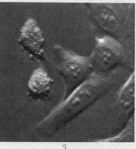

Image 1 was taken 2 hours and 20 minutes after radiation. At 3 hours and 20 minutes, Image 2 shows the cells beginning to "round up" and in Image 3, at 3 hours and 50 minutes, the cells begin to "bleb." Membrane blebbing is when the membrane "boils."

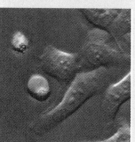

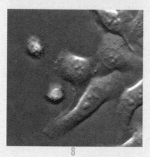

In Images 6 and 7, the membrane is almost completely broken down. Image 8, taken eight hours after radiation, shows both cells in the final stages of death.

When p53 is built right and functioning properly, it stops tumors in their tracks. Radiation therapy can pick up where natural defenses leave off. Radiation kills cancer cells, but not directly. Instead it cause major breaks in DNA. The damage activates p53, causing cancer cells to destroy themselves. Tamoxifen, a drug used to treat breast cancer, uses the p53 route, too.

Any mutation of the p53 gene spells trouble. More than 50 kinds of cancer involve an abnormal p53 gene.[16] Some changes in p53 are inherited, but most arise from envi-ronmental causes, such as cigarette smoke (lung cancer) or the ultraviolet rays of the sun (skin cancer).

University of Iowa researcher Toshinori Hoshi has studied a protein in fruit flies that triggers apoptosis. The protein is aptly named Reaper. "If there isn't enough protein like Reaper to initiate cell death, abnormal cells, like cancer cells, are not destroyed. If there is too much, …[it] kills cells that shouldn't die," Hoshi says.[17] Some researchers think that Alzheimer's disease, which results from the death of brain cells, may actually be a case of apoptosis gone wild. Cancers, on the other hand, may result from a failure of apoptosis, when cells that should commit suicide don't.

Did Jack give up his life for Rose Bukater? Watch *Titanic* to find out. Do your cells die to save you? The fact that you are here, now, reading this book, answers that question.

• • • • •

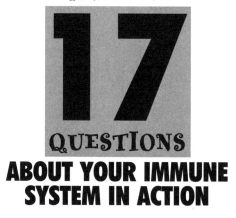

CHAPTER TWO

17 QUESTIONS

ABOUT YOUR IMMUNE SYSTEM IN ACTION

The immune system is the body's doctor, our own personal physician that cures and protects us from a panoply of diseases.

• ROBERT S. DESOWITZ •

Does My Brain Tell My Immune System What to Do?

Yes, and the immune system has a few orders for the brain as well.

Impulses travel along nerve fibers back and forth between the brain and the rest of the body. The impulses signal the brain. They report on conditions in the environment and the status of body systems. If anything changes—either inside or out—the brain triggers a response, whether it's running from danger or eating when hungry. Hormones and cytokines are the chemicals that convey messages to and from the brain, in much the same way. Among their many jobs is control of the numbers and kinds of immune cells.

Three organs make and release hormones that are especially important to the immune system. The hypothalamus and pituitary are glands in the brain. The adrenal glands lie atop the kidneys. Together, these three form the HPA (<u>h</u>ypothalamus, <u>p</u>ituitary, <u>a</u>drenal) axis.

How does the HPA axis work? The organs can inhibit or stimulate each other. The action depends on the kinds and quantities of chemical messengers traveling among them. For example, cytokines from immune cells travel to the hypothalamus in the blood. They can also stimulate nerves to send messages to the brain. Either way, when these messages reach the hypothalamus, they cause it to make hormones that affect the pituitary gland. That can either turn up or turn down the immune system.

Here's only one example among many: The hypothalamus makes a hormone called CRH. CRH causes the pituitary to release another hormone, ACTH. ACTH, in turn, prompts the adrenals to make cortisol. Cortisol is a stress hormone. It depresses the immune system. It's good when it prevents the immune system from overreacting and destroying healthy tissue. It's bad when stress makes you vulnerable to disease.

Does Stress Increase My Chances of Getting Sick?

The stresses of life take a toll on the immune system. Death, divorce, injury, and unemployment are obvious stressors. Less obvious is the stress of happy events such as holidays or vacations. Researchers have created risk tables that predict illness following stressful events. The greater the total number of points, the more likely disease becomes.[1] For example:

Event	Risk points	Event	Risk points
Death of spouse	100	Death of a close friend	37
Divorce	73	Outstanding personal achievement	28
Going to jail	63	Beginning or ending school	26
Death of a close family member	63	Moving	20
Major injury or illness	53	Vacation	13
Getting fired	47	Christmas	12

A major illness or injury adds 53 points to the risk total. That means that one bout of bad health makes another more likely. For example, scientists at Ohio State University studied women after surgery for breast cancer. They found that stress produced a 20 to 30 percent drop in natural killer cells.[2] Another Ohio State team found that stress can lengthen the time that wounds take to heal by as much as 40 percent. Stress also reduces by two-thirds the production of interleukin-1, a cytokine important to the healing process.[3]

Stress can also prompt behaviors that diminish immunity. When the going gets tough, some people head for the refrigerator, the liquor store, or the cigarette machine. They sleep poorly and exercise less. All these behaviors weaken the immune system.

How Does Stress Affect My Immune System?

Think about how your body responds when you get bad news, fail a test, or argue with a friend. You tense, then relax. Your heart pounds. Your mouth goes dry. Butterflies wiggle in your stomach. Your hands get clammy. This is the "fight or flight" state. This involuntary response prepares you to face an attack or run away. In an emergency, you are capable of feats of strength and endurance that you might never have thought possible.

The HPA axis controls the "fight or flight" response. It triggers the release of hormones that cause

- the heart to beat faster, blood pressure to rise, and the pupils to dilate.
- deeper breathing and relaxation of the air tubes that serve the lungs.
- a slowdown in digestion.

- an increase in blood supply to the muscles.
- changes in blood chemistry that make clotting easier should the body be wounded.
- stored fat to change to sugar. (Sugar is the fuel the body needs for quick action.)

At the same time, "fight or flight" hormones slow or stop the immune system. It's as if the body sets priorities. When an external enemy looms, an internal enemy must wait.

Short-term stress is no problem. Your body returns to normal quickly, and the immune system resumes its efforts. But if hormone levels stay high too long, your ability to fight disease drops. Ronald Glaser at Ohio State University gave hepatitis vaccines to 48 students. Twenty-three were in the middle of final exams. Their blood showed high levels of stress hormones. A month later, Glaser tested the students' blood for immunity against hepatitis. Those who had been under stress when they were vaccinated developed the least resistance to hepatitis.[4]

Why Is the Immune Response So Slow?

Maybe it's not. Maybe you're just impatient.

That you recover from food poisoning in a day or a cold in a week is truly remarkable, considering the scale of the operation. Think about the legions of pathogens that must be attacked and destroyed. Consider the complex missions, weapons, and coordination of the different fighting units—the T cells, B cells, and complement. Plasma cells alone handle a heavy workload. They select genes, make proteins, splice molecules together, and manufacture antibodies by the billions. From this point of view, the immune system is a miracle of speed and efficiency.

Does a Newborn Baby Have an Immune System?

Yes, but it's not completely the child's own for several months.

At first, an infant's immunity comes mostly from its mother. During pregnancy, the mother's body makes antibodies against whatever pathogens invade her. She also passes some of her antibodies to her unborn child. The placenta, which nourishes the developing infant, acts as a filter. It won't let large antibodies through, but IgG molecules are relatively small. They pass freely through the placental barrier and enter the baby's blood. At birth, the infant actually has a higher concentration of IgG antibodies in its blood than are present in the mother's blood.

The development of the infant's immune system begins before birth. Between conception and about the eleventh week, a yolk sac nourishes the embryo. Stem cells that create blood cells line the walls of the sac. Later, when the yolk sac disappears, the stem cells travel to the developing bone marrow. There they continue making both red and white blood cells.

The womb is a sterile environment, but occasionally infections can sneak in. Around the fifth month of pregnancy, the fetus can make its own IgG and IgA antibodies if necessary. If a mother catches measles, for example, the fetus will produce antibodies against the virus.

Complement, that series of enzymes that digests invaders, does not come from the mother. The fetus makes its own, although complement does not function fully until two or three months after birth. By then both the bone marrow and the thymus work well, too.

Does Breast-feeding Strengthen a Baby's Immune System?

If a pathogen invades the mother, she produces antibodies that fight it. Some antibodies pass to the child in breast milk. This system is specific and efficient. No energy is wasted. Both mother and child get only the antibodies they need. Most of the antibodies in breast milk are IgA. The baby's digestive enzymes don't break it down. IgA has another advantage. It prevents disease without causing allergic reactions, as IgE often does.

Antibodies aren't the only immune protection a mother shares with her infant:

- Neutrophils and macrophages in breast milk consume harmful bacteria.
- Breast milk produced in the first few days after birth contains a large amount of the virus-killing cytokine, interferon.
- Immune cells and chemicals in breast milk stimulate the infant's immune system to develop.
- Sugar molecules in mother's milk attach to the lining of the baby's digestive tract. They prevent pathogens from crossing into the infant's bloodstream.
- A protein called lactoferrin in breast milk hooks onto iron atoms. That limits the growth of pathogens that need iron. Another chemical in breast milk binds to vitamin B12 with a similar result.
- Breast milk encourages the growth of beneficial bacteria in the baby's stomach and intestines.

Can a Person Who Isn't Sick Give a Disease to Others?

Yes. Such people are called carriers. Some of their stories have sad endings.

Perhaps the most famous carrier of a disease was Mary Mallon.[5] Mary was born in 1869 in County Tyrone, Ireland. In her early teens she emigrated to the United States. Mary's robust good health hid a danger she did not understand.

"Typhoid" Mary Mallon threatens George Soper, the epidemiologist whose trail ended at her doorstep.

Mary gave typhoid to perhaps 50 people during her lifetime. Three of them died. She infected them with *Bacillus typhosus*, the rod-shaped bacteria that cause typhoid. The bacteria travel from person to person in contaminated food or water. The source is the feces or urine of a person who either has the disease or carries the bacteria. Anywhere from one to three weeks after ingesting the bacteria, the symptoms of typhoid appear. They include fever, headache, listlessness, loss of appetite, constipation, and spots on the body. If untreated, one in ten typhoid victims will die. Perhaps 2 to 5 percent of survivors become carriers.[6] That means they carry the bacteria in their bodies without being sick themselves. Mary was a carrier.

On August 4, 1906, Mary went to work as a cook for a wealthy New York banker, Charles Henry Warren. He and his family rented a summerhouse at Oyster Bay on Long Island. Less than a month later, six of the eleven members of the household had typhoid. The landlord, fearing blame, hired George Soper, an epidemiologist and engineer, to trace the source of the outbreak. Soper followed a trail of clues to Mary.

The New York City Health Commissioner exiled Mary to North Brother Island. There she lived by herself in a small bungalow. She stayed there until 1910, when the commissioner took pity on her. Accepting her promise that she would not handle other people's food ever again, he set her free.

Once liberated, she took the name Mary Brown and went to work again—as a cook! In 1914 she caused a fresh outbreak of typhoid in Newfoundland, New Jersey, and perhaps another in Marblehead, Massachusetts. In 1915 she infected 20 people at New York's Sloane Hospital for Women where she worked in the kitchen. The police arrested Mary. This time she was exiled to North Brother Island for good. She lived alone there for 23 years until her death.

Today, carriers are treated less harshly than was Typhoid Mary, but care must be taken to ensure that they do not spread infection. In the United States, health departments enforce strict rules about employment and sanitation. Carriers sign pledges that they will not work with food or contaminate the water supply. Many must receive permission to move to a new house or town.

Typhoid isn't the only disease that healthy carriers spread. Hepatitis C carriers can pass the disease onto others without knowing it. Apparently healthy people spread the AIDS virus in the early years of their infection, long before the outer signs of AIDS appear. Other sexually transmitted diseases, including herpes and gonorrhea, are often spread by carriers who show no symptoms themselves but are capable of infecting their partners.

Yes. One of the biggest dangers is the sun. The sun's ultraviolet (UV) rays kill helper T cells. With too few helpers around to increase an immune response, antigen-presenting cells stimulate suppressor T cells instead. That turns down antibody production and makes you susceptible to skin cancers and infections.

Some reports hint that infectious diseases occur more frequently in polluted areas. For example, scientists in the former Soviet Union studied children in villages polluted with pesticides. They found abnormal T cell counts and two to five times more lung infections among those children than among children living in cleaner areas.[7] How pesticides alter immunity is unclear. Some seem to change antibody structure. Others may depress T-cell functions.

Some scientists think that low-dose exposure to air and water pollutants poses serious danger. A representative for the National Institute of Environmental Health Science estimates that most people have lost about five percent of their disease-fighting ability due to just one pollutant, polychlorinated biphenyls (or PCBs). Five percent may not sound like much, but in the entire population—including infants, the sick, and the elderly—it could mean millions of illnesses and deaths each year.[8] "We're probably all—and I mean the whole doggone planet—immunosuppressed," says Steve Holladay, an immunologist at Virginia-Maryland Regional College of Veterinary Medicine.[9]

Others think the risk should not be exaggerated. "Your immune system is being assaulted at all times during the day and night, but most of us go through life relatively healthy," says Peter Thomas of Chicago's IIT Laboratories.[10]

Just in case you need another reason to avoid them, tobacco and illegal drugs are immune suppressors.

Lung cancer alone kills 125,000 Americans every year. Emphysema and chronic bronchitis add another 90,000 to the toll.[11] But long before the end comes, smoking cripples the immune defenses of the lungs. Smokers suffer more colds, flu, and pneumonia than nonsmokers do. So do the nonsmokers nearby.

Drug smokers experience a 60 percent loss of the disease-fighting ability of their lungs.[12] Smoking marijuana or cocaine paralyzes the macrophages that destroy bacteria in the tiny air sacs of the lungs. Marijuana users have precancerous cells in their air tubes and inflammation in their lungs. Smoking also paralyzes the hairlike cells that line the airways and sweep out invaders.

In small amounts, alcohol probably does little harm to adults. However, heavy drinking—even occasionally—spells disaster for the immune system.

Virtually all immune functions are decreased in alcoholics and alcohol abusers. Alcohol blocks cell-mediated immunity. That may explain why drinkers develop some cancers more often than nondrinkers do. Binge drinking diminishes the number of natural killer cells. Alcohol retards neutrophils, leading to deaths from pneumonia and tuberculosis. Alcohol causes a persistent release of cytokines that can lead to liver failure. Alcohol can also provoke an autoimmune disease of the liver, in which antibodies attack liver tissue.

Why Do I Catch a Cold Every Time I Gt Wet and Chilled?

For decades, scientists have scoffed at mother's advice, "Dress warm so you don't get a cold." Viruses cause colds, not bad weather, they said. Now, new findings suggest that mother is at least partly right—although the debate is far from over.

The new idea goes like this. Sudden or severe cold is a source of stress. The body responds with adrenaline (also called epinephrine), a hormone made by the adrenal gland that initiates the "fight or flight" response. While all other systems swing into high gear, the immune system slows. Fewer T cells, B cells, and antibodies are made. Since cold viruses are so common, your body has probably been fighting them all along, and you haven't been aware of it. So the shutdown of the immune system gives the viruses the advantage. Your body loses the battle and you get a cold—just because you left home without your jacket.

Nevertheless, chilly, wet weather alone cannot give you a cold. It takes a virus. Without a virus, you'll stay cold-free—rain or shine.

Why Do I Sleep More Mhen I'm Sick?

When you are fighting an infection, the brain triggers your sleep centers. While you sleep, your pituitary gland sends out commands to step up leukocyte production. It's not your imagination that you can go to bed sick and wake up well.

Why Do Doctors Take White Blood Counts When I'm Sick?

When you're sick, the bone marrow and thymus speed up production of T cells and B cells. Large numbers of lymphocytes fight equally large numbers of pathogens. The number of white cells in your blood is a good indicator of how sick you are and how well your immune system is working.

Doctors can also count the numbers and types of immune cells to help make a diagnosis. For example, certain bacterial infections cause the number of neutrophils to increase.

Is Exercise Good for My Immune System?

Yes, to a point. People who exercise at least once a week show higher T cell functions than those who don't. Exercise reduces the levels of stress hormones in the blood. It speeds up the manufacture and maturation of immune cells. An hour of aerobic exercise raises levels of interferons and interleukin-1 in the blood. Even five minutes of moderate exertion promotes the action of natural killer cells.

David Nieman at Loma Linda University studied people over the age of sixty-five. Some of them had been exercising for an average of 90 minutes a day for 12 years or more. Others of the same age were sedentary and overweight. Nieman found that T cells and natural killer cells functioned more than 50 percent better in the fit people.[13]

Too much of a good thing, however, can spell trouble. Nieman tested 2,300 runners who registered for the 1987 Los Angeles marathon. About 13 percent of those who were healthy at the time of the race reported a cold a week later. Only 2 percent of those who trained but didn't run the race got a cold. Runners who ran more than 60 miles (96 km) a week doubled their odds of respiratory infection. Stress hormones—especially cortisol—rise to very high levels for several hours after a marathon. "Your immune system is under stress, and this allows the virus to gain a foothold. Not only marathoners but runners who over-train also weaken their immune system," Nieman says.[14]

For professional and competitive athletes, the colds and flu that accompany overtraining are probably unavoidable. One bit of medical advice should never be ignored, however. Don't work out if you have the flu. In a few cases, people have died from exercising vigorously while fighting a viral infection.

Do Certain Foods Boost Immunity? To fight disease, the body needs vitamins A, B, C, E, and folic acid. It also needs the minerals iron, zinc, selenium, and copper. Although we know that deficiencies of these substances hinder immune functions, we don't know exactly what vitamins and minerals do in a healthy immune system.

Many people take extra vitamin C when they catch a cold, but whether it helps is unproven. It's true that vitamin C accumulates in immune cells. This happens because growth factors—proteins that stimulate the production and development of immune cells—also cause cells to take up more glucose. Glucose is a simple sugar, the cell's source of energy. The same sites on the cell's surface that let glucose in also let vitamin C in. How this affects immunity—if it does at all—remains a mystery.

Some people claim that particular foods or herbs boost immunity, but little hard evidence exists. Beware of headlines that promise "super foods to keep you well all winter." Foods such as yogurt, garlic, broccoli, and orange juice are good for you. But loading up on a small number of foods and failing to eat a balanced diet does more harm than good. "There's no one food or group of foods that is going to be better than others," says immunologist Ranjit Chandra.[15]

Weight-loss diets can spell trouble for the immune system. David Nieman found that losing less than a kilogram (1.5 pounds) per week

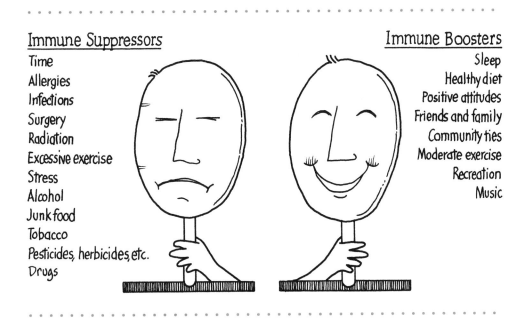

Immune Suppressors

Time
Allergies
Infections
Surgery
Radiation
Excessive exercise
Stress
Alcohol
Junk food
Tobacco
Pesticides, herbicides, etc.
Drugs

Immune Boosters

Sleep
Healthy diet
Positive attitudes
Friends and family
Community ties
Moderate exercise
Recreation
Music

suppressed both T cells and natural killer cells.[16] A diet lacking protein can lead to low levels of T cells and antibodies. Too little folic acid in the diet depresses T cell numbers. A deficiency of vitamins B1 and B2 lowers B cell activity.

The best advice has been around for a long time. Eat a balanced diet that's low in fat and high in nutrients. Limit sugars. Eat more whole grains and fish. Most important, eat a lot of fruits and vegetables. People who do cut their cancer risk in half.[17]

Can Beliefs Affect My Immune System?

Some people think the "placebo effect" proves that expectations can heal. The effect shows up nearly every time that a drug or experimental treatment is tested. To study drug action fairly, researchers divide their subjects into two groups. One group receives the experimental drug. The other receives a placebo or "sugar pill" that should have no effect on the illness. Participants don't know which group they are in. Not even their doctors know. Nevertheless, more than one in three of those who take the placebo get better.[18]

Why? Maybe they would have improved without treatment. Maybe getting treatment changed their attitude toward the illness. They don't get any better, but they aren't as worried. Or maybe their belief in the treatment stimulates the immune system.

The first evidence of a genuine immune response to a placebo came in 1975 from Robert Ader and Nicholas Cohen at the University of Rochester in New York. They mixed into sweet water a drug that slows the immune response and gave the mixture to rats. The drug worked as expected. The immune response slowed. The surprise came when the same rats got sweet water without the drug. Their immune responses slowed, too, although the drug was not present. Somehow, the rats' brains dampened the immune system in response to sweet water alone.

If rats can display such complex associations, what are humans capable of? According to the American Psychological Association, optimism is a potent force for good health. Psychologists at the University of California Los Angeles measured confidence and fear among first-year law students. The students showed no differences in their immune systems before school began. By mid-semester, the optimistic students had higher counts of both natural killer and helper T cells than did their pessimistic peers.

What Can I Do to Strengthen My Immune System?

While you may be tired of hearing the rules of good health, they remain your best defense against disease. Sleep, eat right, exercise, and avoid tobacco, drugs, and alcohol. Attitudes are important too. Think positive. Keep your life in balance with work, rest, and play.

Beyond that, some tools for building a strong immune system can be downright fun. Francis Brannaf at Wilkes University in Wilkes-Barre, Pennsylvania, recommends "easy listening" music. In one experiment, 30 minutes of Muzak raised the level of antibodies in saliva by 14 percent. Radio jazz interrupted by weather reports and traffic message produced only half that gain. Silence had no effect, but clicking noises sent IgA levels plummeting by 20 percent.[19]

Humor is another option. In 1990, Herbert Lefcourt, a professor at the University of Waterloo in Ontario, Canada, measured levels of IgA in the saliva of 41 college students. Antibody levels rose among students who listened to humorous tapes. Antibody levels stayed the same among those who listened to a class lecture. Lee Berk at Loma Linda University in California says, "Laughter is hazardous to your illness." He found that humorous videos increase killer cell activity and double the amount of gamma interferon in blood plasma.[20]

Finally, the best defense against disease may be good friends, family, and neighbors. Researchers at the University of Pittsburgh Medical School studied "social roles"—the relationships of their test subjects with other people. They found that people reporting many social roles were less likely to get sick than people having only a few. "Although chicken soup may provide soothing relief to cold symptoms, it is the friend who brings you the soup that is proving to be important in maintaining health."[21]

Is the Cleanest Defense a Dirty Offense?

. . . . .

Give us this day our daily germs.

G.A.W. ROOK

. . . . .

Writer Phil Williams calls bacteria "the huddled masses of the microbial world." How important are these huddled masses, all five million trillion trillion of them![22]

Consider these facts:

- Somewhere between 80 and 90 percent of the living matter on earth is microbes.
- Within seconds after birth, about 400 kinds of microorganisms have taken up residence in or on a baby's body.
- More bacteria live in your gut than the total number of people who have ever lived.[23]

- Your mouth is home to more than 600 species of microbes.
- You have 10 to 100 times more microbes on or in your body than you have cells.

As large as these numbers sound, they pose a lesser threat than you might think. Most bacteria are harmless. Others are beneficial. Bacteria that live in your digestive tract help digest food and build important vitamins. They extract nutrients from fibrous foods, providing you with extra food energy. Perhaps most important, they protect you against pathogens. With a healthy population of harmless or beneficial bacteria well established, it's hard for a pathogen to gain a foothold.

Human pathogens make up less than 1 percent of the microbe total, yet we go to great lengths to destroy them. "We can now wipe our antibacterial cutting board with an antibacterial sponge, shower with antibacterial soap, and sleep beneath an antibacterial quilt on an antibacterial pillow," writes Garry Hamilton in the *New Scientist*.[24]

Dr. Graham Rook of the University College, London, says we shouldn't be so careful about avoiding germs. Throughout human history, he argues, children have been exposed to dirt and microbes from the moment of birth. That encounter with foreign agents may be essential to the development of the immune system. In today's squeaky-clean homes, the immune system encounters too little dirt to develop properly, Rook says.

Rook says the problem lies in alternative paths for helper T cell development. T cells can develop and mature by either of two routes, which he calls Th1 and Th2. Those that develop through the Th1 pathway are the immune system's most powerful weapons against disease. They make cytokines that signal the system to swing into action. They release chemicals that kill macrophages that are overloaded with infectious agents.

In a normal immune system, Th2 lymphocytes play a more limited role. They work best in fighting worms and large parasites. They also release chemicals that trigger the production of IgE antibodies. IgE is to blame for many allergies. It causes cells to release histamine. Histamine stimulates a flood of mucus. The flood is good when it helps wash parasites away from stomach walls. It's not much help, however, when it's happening in your nose or lungs. Then we call it hay fever or asthma.

Rook thinks the "balance of power" should be tipped in favor of Th1. In childhood, T cells are "naïve"—another way of saying that they have not yet "learned" to mature into either Th1 or Th2 cells. Dirt—or more correctly, organisms in dirt called *Mycobacteria*—stimulate the development of Th1 cells, in Rook's view. In the absence of *Mycobacteria*, too many cells become the Th2 variety, he says. Allergies, asthma, and autoimmune diseases result.

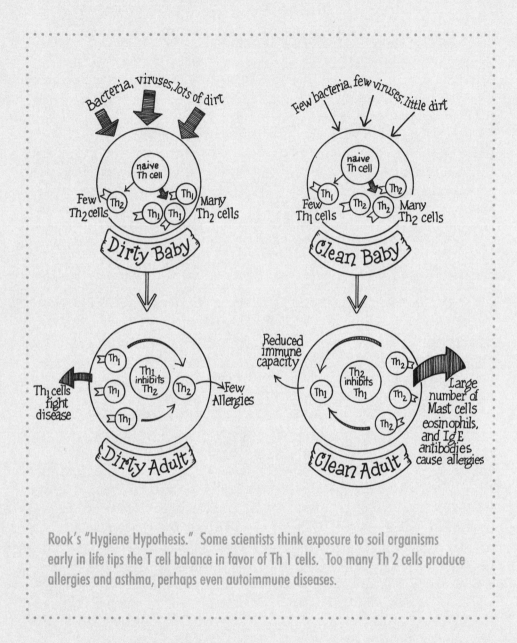

Rook's "Hygiene Hypothesis." Some scientists think exposure to soil organisms early in life tips the T cell balance in favor of Th 1 cells. Too many Th 2 cells produce allergies and asthma, perhaps even autoimmune diseases.

Professor Stephen Holgate of Southampton University in England sees merit in Rook's ideas. Asthma rates are rising rapidly in the United States, Western Europe, Japan, and Australia. Allergies are also becoming more common in industrialized nations. Asthma and allergies are rare in Africa and much of Asia where hygiene standards are far looser. So maybe, says one reporter, "Getting ill in the short term can be good for you in the long run."[25]

In 1989, British scientist David Strachan reported his study of 17,000 children born in March 1958. He followed their health for 23 years.[26] Those most likely to suffer from hay fever came from the smallest families. Older children had more allergies than their younger brothers and sisters. Strachan thinks early childhood infections reduce the risk of allergies. In Strachan's opinion, older children and those from smaller families were less likely to derive the "benefits" of having many infections.

Rook's and Strachan's arguments have failed to convince many experts. Doctors point out that children who live in dirty inner-city environments have higher rates of asthma than do children from the cleaner suburbs. Rook responds that inner-city children rarely come into contact with soil organisms. "The inner-city guys don't have gardens," he says.[27]

Others argue that natural variability among individuals may explain some observed patterns. For example, perhaps those children who get measles and recover inherited stronger immune systems to begin with. Even David Strachan admits that no direct evidence proves that childhood diseases prevent allergies.

While not even Rook would suggest that we all eat dirt, he and his colleagues are working on a new vaccine derived from *Mycobacterium*. They hope the vaccine will prevent or treat asthma by stimulating the Th1 system.

• • • • •

CHAPTER THREE

QUESTIONS

ABOUT
INFECTIOUS DISEASES

There is no single problem that is more pressing than
our fast-deteriorating relations with the microbial world.

• BARBARA CULLITON •

Aren't Infectious Diseases a Thing of the Past?

Hardly. Infectious diseases are the leading cause of death worldwide. In the United States, they take 160,000 lives each year.[1]

"Infectious diseases are humankind's oldest and most persistent enemy," said Alan F. Holmer in 1998, while serving as president of the Pharmaceutical Research and Manufacturers of America.[2] That same year, a survey disclosed that 78 medical research and drug companies were testing nearly 140 potential new weapons in the battle against pathogens, including new vaccines, antibiotics, and antiviral drugs.

What Kinds of
Microbes Cause
Disease?

Disease-causing microbes are parasites; they depend on another organism for all or part of their life support. Viruses are total parasites. They reproduce only when infecting a living cell. Pathogenic bacteria, such as the kind of *Streptococcus* that causes sore throats, are occasional parasites. When they are not infecting a body, they survive in a dormant state. Other examples of part-time pathogens include certain protozoa, fungi, roundworms, and flatworms.

When a virus attaches to a living cell, it dissolves a hole in the cell's membrane and injects its DNA or RNA into the host cell. The genetic material of the virus seizes control of the cell and sets it to making viruses. Instead of operating to maintain the life of the host organism, the cell becomes a virus-making factory. Viruses can reproduce at a

The strain of *Streptococcus* bacteria that causes sore throats: on the left, in its active, growing state; on the right, in its encapsulated, dormant state.

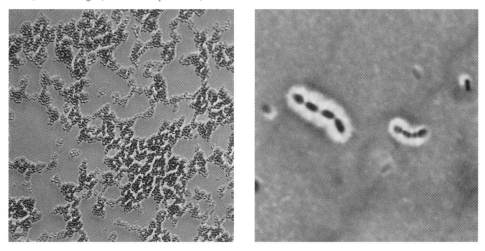

phenomenal rate. In 12 hours, a single virus can give rise to 10^{73} (a 1 with 73 zeroes after it) copies of itself.[3]

Unlike viruses, bacteria have a life of their own. They take food from the host organism and use it to support their own life functions. They release waste products that are toxic to their host. Some bacteria do their damage directly, by killing the cells they invade. Others cause disease indirectly through the poisonous waste products they release.

Some protozoa, fungi, roundworms, and flatworms parasitize the human body. Each has its unique way of wreaking havoc. For example, *Plasmodium*, the organism that causes malaria, hides from the immune

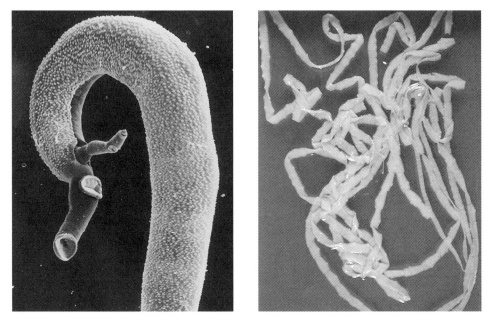

The schistosome fluke, left, lays eggs that can damage the human liver, intestines, lungs, and bladder. When not infecting people, the fluke lives in freshwater snails. This tapeworm, right, taken from an adult, is more than 32 feet (10 meters) long. Tapeworms can cause diarrhea, increased appetite and general weakness.

system inside red blood cells. It reproduces there. The cell dies when it bursts and releases more parasites. If unchecked, the *Plasmodium* enters and kills more and more red blood cells. Finally, too few remain to carry enough food and oxygen to the body's tissues. The result is weakness, fever, and other symptoms of malaria.

Fungi look and act a lot like plants, but they cannot make their own food. They take food from another source. Fungi that live on dead and waste materials perform a valuable service to the environment. They decompose carbon compounds and return the elements to the cycle of life. Other fungi are parasites on the human body. Athlete's foot, ringworm (misnamed; it's not a worm!), and yeast infections are caused by fungi.

Are Any Pathogens Big Enough to See? Get a tapeworm in your gut and it can grow a meter (3 feet) or more in length. That's longer than the distance from your nose to the tip of your fingers. At about a centimeter (0.4 inch) long, the schistosome fluke is one one-hundredth that size. At that length it's big enough to see. If you look closely, you might also see microfilaria, tiny worms (about a half-millimeter long) that circulate in the bloodstream. Mosquitoes spread them.

The pathogens in the chart below are in the minority. Most are too small to see without a light microscope or an electron microscope.[4]

Microscope Range	Pathogen	Approximate Size
Light	*Ameba* (causes dysentery)	0.02 millimeter *or* 2×10^{-5} meter
Light	*Mycobacterium tuberculosis*	0.003 millimeter *or* 3×10^{-6} meter
Electron	Variola virus (smallpox)	0.0007 millimeter *or* 7×10^{-7} meter
Electron	Poliovirus	0.00001 millimeter *or* 1×10^{-8} meter

It will be many years before scientists can answer that question fully, but research points to
some of the ways that viruses:

• block or inactivate interferon, the virus-
  killing cytokine.
• make proteins that prevent formation of T cells and B cells.
• block the production of proteins that trigger apoptosis (see page 42).
• release growth factors that cause infected cells to multiply rapidly
  (thus multiplying viruses faster than the immune system can fight
  back).
• produce chemicals that suppress the immune system.
• discharge proteins that block complement.

Ulcers are sores in the stomach or intestines
that do not heal. A person's diet or disposition
formerly was thought to cause ulcers. Spicy
foods got the blame. People with ulcers were
said to be high-strung, nervous, and easily upset. Doctors prescribed
relaxation, antacids, and a bland diet for the three million Americans
with ulcers.[5]

Then researchers found a bacterium, *Helicobacter pylori*, in the stom-
achs of most people with ulcers. Many ulcer patients improved as soon
as they begin taking antibiotics. Doctors who had long assumed that
ulcers came from personality or lifestyle had to change their view. In
1994 a panel of the National Institutes of Health recommended antibiotics for ulcer patients.

The hypothalamus in the brain controls body temperature. It works like a thermostat, sensing the temperature of your blood. When you're well, it maintains homeostasis. Your body temperature varies a little around 98.6° F (37° C), whether you're sweating in a steam room or hiking in the Yukon.

When a pathogen invades, your body needs time to identify antigens and produce matching antibodies. In the meantime, more general weapons combat the enemy. The immune system sends chemical messages to the hypothalamus signaling the need for a rise in body temperature. In response, the hypothalamus causes the pituitary to release a hormone called TSH (thyroid stimulating hormone).

TSH travels through the blood and reaches the thyroid gland in the neck. There, it stimulates the thyroid to make another hormone, thyroxine. Thyroxine travels to all the cells of the body. It makes them burn food faster, generating more heat. The result is a fever. Many pathogens can't survive high temperatures, so the fever kills them.

As the pathogen begins to lose the battle, other chemical messengers travel to the hypothalamus. The hypothalamus signals the pituitary. TSH production decreases, thyroxine levels decrease, and body cells release energy more slowly. Your temperature returns to normal.

There's a lot more to a fever than a change in temperature. Researchers find high levels of immune chemicals, including interleukins 6 and 10 and interferon-gamma, in people with fevers. When healthy volunteers took IL-6 in a research project, they got fevers and flulike symptoms.[6] Treatments that reduce the levels of cytokines alleviate the symptoms. This suggests that cytokines not only fight illness but also produce some of its symptoms, including fever.

How the immune system triggers a fever.

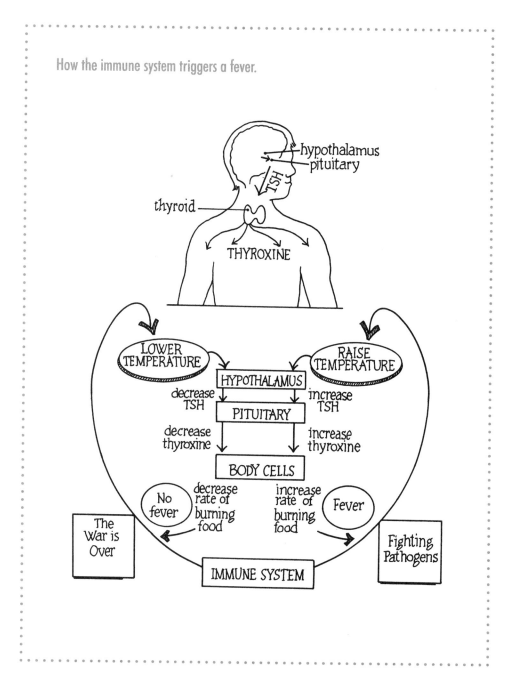

How Do Antibiotics Work?

Different antibiotics work in different ways. Some examples:

- Penicillin: stops bacteria from constructing their cell walls.
- Erythromycin: interferes with the ability of certain bacteria to manufacture proteins.
- Trimethoprim: prevents bacteria from making DNA.

We usually think of antibiotics as pills sold in bottles, but the body produces natural antibiotics of its own. Human beta-defensin-2 (HBD-2), for example, is a small protein that kills bacteria on the skin. It works by punching holes in the membranes of the bacteria. Another antibiotic is HBD-1. It protects against bladder infections. It reaches high levels in the urine of pregnant women. Some scientists suspect that people who have frequent bladder infections may make too little HBD-1.

What's Bad About Taking Too Many Antibiotics?

Antibiotics kill all bacteria, not just the ones that make you sick. That includes the beneficial bacteria that help keep the digestive tract healthy. That's why antibiotics often cause diarrhea. It's also why antibiotics should be taken only in small doses for short periods of time. Complete annihilation of beneficial bacteria can allow pathogens to cross the wall of the stomach and intestines and enter the bloodstream.

If Antibiotics Don't Work Why Do Doctors Prescribe Them?

The Institute of Medicine reported in 1998 that up to half of all prescriptions for antibiotics are unnecessary.[7] Doctors grab their prescription pads to silence demanding patients who aren't satisfied with the "rest and drink fluids" advice. People who expect a "magic pill" for every sniffle are misinformed. The only cure for a cold or flu is time.

In more severe cases—such as viral pneumonia—doctors may prescribe antibiotics to prevent "secondary" infections. That's when a system already weakened in the battle against a virus falls prey to a bacterial infection. But even then antibiotics should be prescribed with care. Why? Because taking antibiotics to prevent an illness, rather than treat one, increases chances of developing an antibiotic-resistant strain of microbes. Later, when serious infections come along and antibiotics are really needed, they prove useless.

How Do Pathogens Become Resistant to Antibiotics?

Imagine a population of a million bacterial cells. Among them a mere five—by chance—have a special ability. They make an enzyme that digests the antibiotic, penicillin. Along comes penicillin, which kills all the bacteria except those five.

The survivors become the parents of the next generation. The generation time in human beings is about 25 years. In many bacteria, it's 20 minutes. That means the population doubles three times in one hour. Get out your calculator and convince yourself that the number of bacteria will exceed one million again in only six hours.

This population differs from the original one. Derived from parent cells that could destroy penicillin, these cells are penicillin destroyers, too. They inherited the gene for making the antibiotic-digesting enzyme from the parent stock. All that is needed after that is the spread of the microbe from one host to another. That can happen in the intestines, blood, soil, water, or laboratory—any place that microbes find the warmth, moisture, and food they need to multiply.

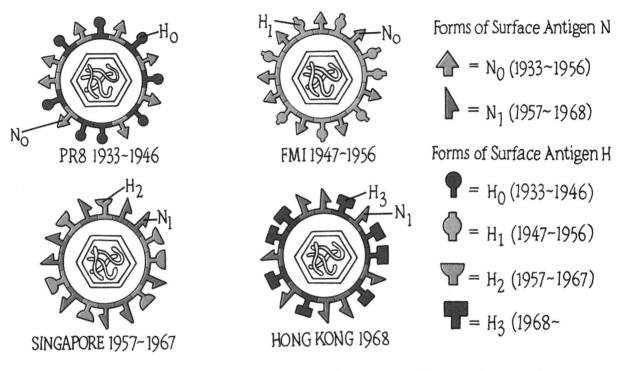

Forms of Surface Antigen N

$\bigwedge$ = N_0 (1933~1956)

$\bigwedge$ = N_1 (1957~1968)

Forms of Surface Antigen H

= H_0 (1933~1946)

= H_1 (1947~1956)

= H_2 (1957~1967)

= H_3 (1968~

PR8 1933~1946

FMI 1947~1956

SINGAPORE 1957~1967

HONG KONG 1968

Mutations of the flu virus: Between 1933 and 1968 the N antigen on the virus surface mutated once. The H antigen mutated three times. Each strain of flu has its own characteristics as a result.

Prescribing antibiotics unnecessarily increases the risk of resistant strains developing. So does the use of antibiotics in agriculture. Farm animals are routinely given antibiotics to keep them well and to increase their production of meat and milk. The result is the development of antibiotic-resistant strains in animals that may "cross over" and infect humans.

Bacteria multiply by dividing. One cell becomes two, two become four, and so on. Each new cell is a copy of the original, but the copying process is never totally accurate. Chance mutations occur. Sometimes mistakes are made as the genetic material DNA (or sometimes RNA in a virus) is copied. Although many of these errors harm the cell, a few may turn out to be beneficial, such as a mutation that leads to antibiotic resistance.

Microbes also get changed genetic material from other microbes. When a bacterial cell dies, pieces of its DNA spill out into its environment. Some of these pieces pass through the outer membranes of other cells. Once inside, they can join with the genetic material of their new host. This process, called transformation, gives the recipient some of the characteristics of the donor.

Another source of change is the bacteriophage. Bacteriophages are viruses that infect bacteria. They can transplant their own DNA or DNA from another organism into a new host cell. Yet another way of spreading antibiotic resistance is the plasmid. Plasmids are rings of DNA that lie outside the nucleus of the bacteria. Plasmids can easily migrate from one kind of bacteria to another, sometimes taking with them mutant genes that confer antibiotic resistance.

The Mayo Clinic recommends these steps:

- Don't insist on antibiotics when your doctor says "No."
- Never keep unfinished prescriptions to use later.
- Never share antibiotics with others.
- Keep a record of your prescriptions and inform your doctor.
- Take your pills for the full time prescribed.

That last piece of advice merits explanation. Stopping a course of antibiotics too soon allows the hardiest bacteria to survive and reproduce. That increases the chances of selecting a resistant population. So even if you feel better, take all the pills in the bottle. You'll do yourself (and the world) a favor.

Is It True That Flesh-eating Bacteria Devour a Person

The misleading name "flesh-eating bacteria" arose when a British newspaper printed the sensational headline, "Killer Bug Ate My Face." "I hate that [term]," says Vincent Fischetti of Rockefeller University. "I picture Pac-Man organisms."[8] The bacteria don't eat flesh, he explains.

It's caused by a type of *Streptococcus*, the same bacteria that cause painful sore throats. The disease begins when the bacteria get into the skin through a cut or scrape. Once inside they produce poisons that turn skin black as connective cells die. The immune system easily handles it in most people long before any damage can be done. But an unfortunate few can't fight off this pathogen.

The condition is treated with antibiotics and surgery to remove dead tissue. Prospects are good if it is spotted early. If the poison gets into the bloodstream, the patient may die.

Could Ebola Really Wipe Out the Human Population?

The Ebola virus is a filovirus. It is shaped like a worm with a hook at the end. It was named in 1976 when a deadly, bleeding fever broke out among the people of the Ebola River, a tributary of the Congo in Zaire. Ebola is one among several deadly hemorrhagic fevers that kill through severe bleeding.

The Zaire strain of Ebola kills 90 percent of those infected by it. Death is swift—usually within 48 hours of infection.[9] A virus that lethal could easily kill millions of people quickly, much as did the Black Death of the Middle Ages. So far, Ebola has not wiped out entire populations as the plague did. Three reasons account for the difference:

- Contact with blood or body fluids spreads Ebola. The virus cannot survive in air. (If it could, a cough in a crowded room would be sufficient to set off an epidemic.)
- Recent outbreaks have occurred in rural areas. In cities, the numbers of dead and dying would grow rapidly.
- Ebola kills so swiftly that sick people have little chance to travel and spread the infection. (Nevertheless, an infected person could easily fly from Brazzaville in the Republic of Congo to New York City before showing symptoms of the disease. Spread of an epidemic by air travel is a hazard not to be taken lightly.)

Where the virus hides between outbreaks is still uncertain. Some people think that Ebola, like the AIDS virus, probably originated in chimps or monkeys. It may reside there harmlessly until a transfer infection to humans occurs. Rodents harbor some of the other hemorrhagic fever viruses, including Lassa, Machupo, and Junin fevers and the American hantavirus. (See "Showdown at Muerta Canyon," page 87.)

What Is AIDS and How Is It Treated?

AIDS stands for Acquired Immune Deficiency Syndrome:

- Acquired—the result of a virus that enters the body.
- Immune Deficiency—a loss of the ability to fight off disease.
- Syndrome—a group of signs and symptoms that occur together.

The virus that causes AIDS is the <u>H</u>uman <u>I</u>mmunodeficiency <u>V</u>irus, or HIV. HIV infects helper T cells (also called CD4 cells or T4 cells). Healthy people usually have 600 to 1,200 helper T cells in every microliter of their blood. When that count drops below 200 in people infected with HIV, the body can no longer fight infections. Because helper Ts regulate so many immune functions, HIV effectively shuts down the immune system. AIDS patients die from rare diseases and cancers that seldom strike people with normal immune responses.

Since the early 1980s, scientists have been looking for ways to stop HIV. Drugs slow the progression of the disease and let people with AIDS live longer, healthier lives. The best-known AIDS drug is AZT (azidothymidine). AZT interferes with the multiplication of the virus.

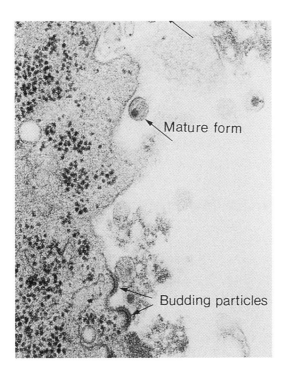

Mature form

Budding particles

This image shows HIV budding from a lymphocyte.

Another class of antiviral drugs called protease inhibitors caused much excitement in the mid-1990s. Protease is an enzyme that HIV uses when building its protein coat. Blocking protease stops the virus from copying itself.

When taken in combination with AZT and other antiviral drugs, protease inhibitors can clear as much as 99 percent of HIV from the blood. Although these drug combinations help many people slow the progression of the disease, they do not cure it. The virus remains in the body and continues to invade and destroy the immune system.

How Do HIV Tests Work?

The only way to find out about an HIV infection is to have a blood test. The test looks not for the virus (that's too difficult and expensive) but for antibodies against it. The test involves sending a sample of blood to a laboratory. For many years, tests had to be arranged through health departments, doctors' offices, or clinics. Now at-home tests are available.

A negative result means that no HIV antibodies were found in the blood. That result does not rule out the possibility of infection. Antibodies can take three months or more after infection to show up. Also, because no test is perfect, a negative result cannot guarantee the absence of HIV. To be safe, doctors recommend repeating the test in a few months and avoiding the behaviors that made HIV infection a risk in the first place.

Why Don't Antibodies Against HIV Work?

Maybe they do. Maybe it's just a matter of numbers.

Scientists once believed that HIV was inactive in the early years of the infection. Now they know better. HIV manufactures billions of copies of itself long before symptoms appear. In 1995 researchers in New York and Alabama reported that the immune system can clear as many as half of the viruses from the blood in only two days. The trouble is that the virus multiplies even more quickly—some 100 billion new viral particles every day. The body defends itself by replacing between 1 and 2 billion helper T cells daily, but that's not enough to keep up.[10]

Sadly, this fight-back response only helps the virus along, giving it more T cells to infect. To explain what's happening, David Ho of the Aaron Diamond AIDS Research Center in New York proposed a "sink model" for helper T cell loss. He compares the immune system's production of new cells to an open tap, constantly filling a sink. Their destruction by HIV is like the drain. Over time, the drain lets the contents of the sink out faster than the tap can fill it.

Not everyone agrees with the sink model. Dutch scientists think the decrease in cell numbers comes not from the "open drain" but from the ability of HIV to turn down the tap—that is, interfere with the production of new T cells. Either way, the result is the same. Helper T cell numbers fall dangerously low, and the immune system collapses.

Are Some People Naturally Immune to HIV?

Maybe. Steve Crohn, dubbed by the press as "The Man Who Can't Catch AIDS," was the first person ever found to be genetically resistant to HIV. In 1994, AIDS researchers in Manhattan took a blood sample from Crohn, isolated his white blood cells, and grew millions of them in culture dishes. They then added measured quantities of the AIDS virus. Crohn's cells did not become infected. Investigators increased the number of viruses ten times, a hundred times, a thousand times.

Still, Crohn's cells remained healthy and normal. The question no one could answer was, "Why?"

Researchers everywhere rushed to discover what made Crohn's cells—and those of a few other people like him—impervious to HIV. Impervious turned out to be the correct word. Somehow, the cell membrane of Crohn's cells kept HIV out. Crohn never got AIDS because the virus could not break through the membranes of his helper T cells.

Cell membranes have many proteins on their surfaces that act as "locks." When a molecular "key" fits onto them, they open a channel in the membrane and allow the molecule inside. These channels let in the oxygen, water, and food the cell needs to live. Viruses such as HIV "pick the lock." They display proteins on their surfaces that resemble "key" molecules closely enough to make the channel open.

One such lock on the outside of T cells is a protein called CCR5. Crohn turned out to be missing CCR5 locks (apparently with no ill effects on his health). Few people enjoy the immunity that Crohn possesses, but scientists wonder if a drug that blocks CCR5 could prevent HIV infection in others.

Does Everyone With HIV Get AIDS?

Maybe not. A very few of those who carry the virus survive for many years without developing AIDS symptoms. Doctors call these people long-term nonprogressors. The virus multiplies more slowly in nonprogressors. Their immune systems don't stop the virus, but they do slow it down.

Samples from the lymph nodes of people with AIDS show tissue that is scarred and wasting away. In nonprogressors, the tissue is normal, and the number of helper T cells in the blood drops sharply in the

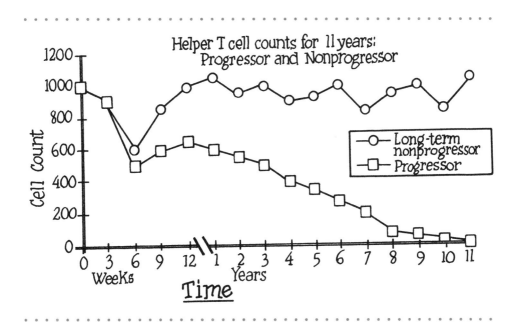

Helper T cell counts for 11 years:
Progressor and Nonprogressor

(Y-axis: Cell Count — 0, 200, 400, 600, 800, 1000, 1200)
(X-axis: Time — Weeks: 0, 3, 6, 9, 12; Years: 1, 2, 3, 4, 5, 6, 7, 8, 9, 10, 11)

Legend:
—○— Long-term nonprogressor
—□— Progressor

early weeks of infection but rises later and remains steady as the years go by. Nonprogressors have large numbers of anti-HIV antibodies in their blood. They also have large numbers of killer T cells.

Can Gene Therapy Cure AIDS?

In theory, it's possible to change the genes in helper T cells so they can resist HIV invasion. In 1996 scientists at the University of Michigan tried. Here's what they did:

- First, they artificially manufactured a gene they thought would interfere with HIV copying itself.

- Next, they separated helper T cells from the blood of three AIDS patients.
- They then used minute particles of gold to "haul" the altered gene into the T cells.
- Finally, they grew large numbers of the altered cells in cultures and returned them to the bodies of their patients.

Later, they found that the altered helper T cells lasted four or five times longer than cells that didn't carry the inserted gene. "This study suggests that gene transfer can be used to prolong T-cell survival and, ultimately, help to sustain the immune system in HIV-infected patients," said Dr. Gary Nabel, a professor at Michigan's Medical Center.[11]

A similar study from the company Cell Genesys, Inc., genetically modified both helper and killer T cells to attack and destroy HIV. Their tests showed that the modified cells survived in the patients' blood. In a majority of test subjects, the modified cells also appeared to reduce the numbers of viruses "hidden" in the lymph tissues of the stomach and intestines.

Another approach might use "suicide genes" to kill infected cells. Tk is a gene that codes for an enzyme called thymidine kinase. The enzyme converts the drug acyclovir into a deadly poison. If the Tk gene could be implanted in cells infected with HIV, then the drug would kill them.

Still another idea depends on a gene that occurs in HIV itself. The gene called Rev controls the production of a protein that HIV needs to replicate. If a defective copy of Rev were introduced into the DNA of T cells, it might cause the production of a defective protein that would stop HIV from multiplying.

These ideas are new and largely untested, and gene therapy poses risks. A transplanted gene could cause cancer or provoke the immune system into attacking itself. Research must be slow and careful.

Can Bone Marrow Transplants Cure Cancer or AIDS?

Every year, 30,000 patients are diagnosed with life-threatening cancers and blood diseases that affect bone marrow.[12] Stem cells in normal bone marrow make all blood cells, including red cells, platelets (important to clotting), and leukocytes. Radiation and chemotherapy (strong anticancer drugs) may kill cancer cells but damage bone marrow at the same time. In such cases, a bone marrow transplant may be the best hope.

Relatives can donate marrow. In some cases, donations from strangers can work. Also promising is research on growing cells from the blood left in umbilical cords after babies are born. Patrick Stiff of Loyola University says stem cells in cord blood are "immunologically naïve. They . . . are more adaptable than mature marrow cells to a new environment."[13] That means a perfect match of antigen types with a donor is not necessary. Umbilical cord cells are frozen and stored in banks throughout the world. With new techniques allowing growth of a large number of cells in as little as 12 days, cord transplants could prove a quick and easy way to save thousands of lives.

In theory, a bone marrow transplant won't help AIDS patients. They have normal bone marrow. It makes T cells just as it should. The problem is that HIV destroys T cells after they are made. It's even possible that a marrow transplant could pass HIV from a donor to a recipient.

But a transplant might work if the donor was not human! Baboons, for example, don't get AIDS. What if a baboon's bone marrow could produce HIV-resistant T cells in the human body? In 1996 doctors transplanted bone marrow from a baboon into AIDS patient Jeff Getty. Would the baboon's bone marrow make T cells to replace Getty's lost ones? The answer was no. The transplant didn't "take." Getty, however, is optimistic that animal-to-human transplants will work in the future. "I'm the first," he told the *San Francisco Chronicle*, "but watch out. There are more coming."[14]

What Infectious Disease Is Most Deadly?

The answer may surprise you.

Worldwide, tuberculosis (TB) is the leading cause of death from an infectious agent.

When a person with TB coughs, tiny droplets carrying *Mycobacterium tuberculosis* spray into the air. The disease spreads when another person breathes in the droplets.

Inside the lung, macrophages ingest the bacteria, but sometimes they are too weak to destroy the invader. When that happens, the bacteria multiply inside immune cells, eventually forming lesions in the lungs called tubercles. Symptoms include coughing blood, fatigue, and difficulty breathing. Tuberculosis can be effectively treated with a nine-month regimen of drugs, but many of the world's poorest people have no access to such medical care.

Showdown at Muerto Canyon

· · · · ·

There's a prowler in the house.

C.J. PETERS
(SPECIAL PATHOGENS BRANCH, CENTERS FOR DISEASE CONTROL)

· · · · ·

Jim Cheek wasn't a police officer. He didn't wear a badge or carry a gun. But on this sunny May morning in 1993, he was heading for a showdown with a killer. Himself a Cherokee Indian, Jim worked as an epidemiologist for the Indian Health Service in New Mexico. That spring morning near Gallup, Cheek set out to investigate a hypothesis. A toxic chemical, he thought, might be responsible for a series of unexplained deaths near Four Corners—the border where four southwestern states meet: Colorado, New Mexico, Arizona, and Utah. So far, five victims had died swiftly and horribly.

Their lungs had filled with plasma (the liquid portion of blood). Gasping for air, they had drowned in their own fluids.

At first, Cheek had thought that the bizarre deaths centered in and near the Navajo Nation might be from a pneumonic plague carried by wild prairie dogs. But the lab had found no plague bacteria in the victims' blood or tissues. Studying hospital records, Cheek suspected that a toxic chemical might be the culprit. Phosgene, a chemical weapon used by Germany during World War I, could produce symptoms such as those that were killing Four Corners

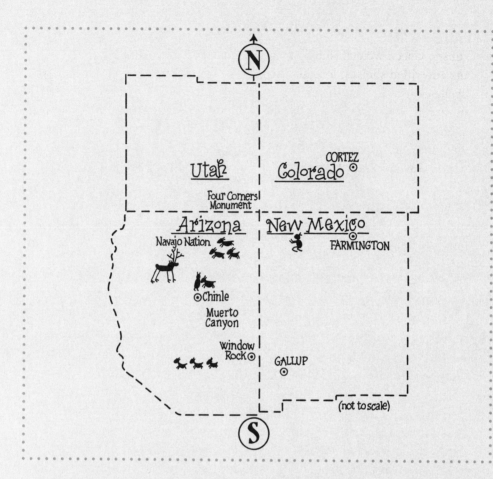

residents. For the most part, phosgene is banned in the United States, but it can be used legally for killing prairie dogs.

Expecting to find phosgene, Cheek drove to the trailer where one of the victims—a long-distance runner named Merrill Bahe—had lived. Sadly, Bahe had died on the way to his girlfriend's funeral. She had died in the same ghastly way.

Never suspecting that the cause of the deaths might still linger in Bahe's trailer, Cheek wore ordinary clothes and shoes—not the protective respirator masks, latex gloves, and biohazard suit and boots often used in his job. He unlocked the trailer and stepped inside. The air smelled dry, dusty. Cheek went through closets and rifled shelves, looking for phosgene canisters, spraying equipment, or chemical residues. He found nothing. Kicking at mouse droppings on the floor, Cheek concluded that rodents had invaded—perhaps after Bahe's death.

If poison wasn't to blame, what was? Bahe had died on May 14, 1993. By May 20, the number of cases totaled ten. Cheek was stumped. Meanwhile, the press had gotten wind of the story. "Mystery Flu Kills Six," read headlines in the *Albuquerque Journal*. Soon other names for the unknown disease were popping up: Sin Nombre (Without a Name); the Navajo disease; the Convict Creek virus.

Cheek turned to the Centers for Disease Control and Prevention in Atlanta, Georgia, for help. "I wondered if it might be some kind of mycoplasma [bacteria], because they're so hard to culture in the laboratory. I thought maybe that's why we weren't finding anything," Cheek said later.[15] At the CDC, scientists tested samples from Four Corners patients against antibodies for every virus they had in stock.

Finally, a match appeared that surprised and puzzled everyone. The Four Corners killer was a virus, a kind of hantavirus. The trouble was that all known hantaviruses occurred

The common deer mouse, carrier of the deadly hanta virus

in Europe and Asia, not in the Americas. They killed by attacking the kidneys, not the lungs. Still, the match was unmistakable

Rodents carry the hantaviruses of the Old World. Was the American form transmitted the same way? Along with Navajo trappers and health workers, three dozen CDC scientists set out for the sites where people had fallen ill. The teams set hundreds of traps. They captured prairie dogs, rats, and skunks, but mostly the brown-and-white deer mouse, *Peromyscus maniculatus*—a charming little creature, "your basic storybook mouse."[16]

Cute or not, the mice turned out to be the carriers. The previously unknown hantavirus turned up in a third of the first 770 mice the CDC tested.[17] The infection must be airborne, they determined. When people stirred up dust from the droppings of an infected mouse—as they might while cleaning a garage or camping out—they breathed in the virus. The aftermath was well documented. The virus multiplied in the lungs, causing tiny blood vessels to leak fluid. Death was swift. Some 70 percent of the virus's victims died within a matter of days.[18]

Although the disease was new to the scientists, the Navajo people had seen it before. Cheek listened to the elders of the tribe. Twice previously in the twentieth century they had seen people die the same way. It always happened, they said, after heavy spring rains. Lots of water makes the piñon pines grow. In such a good season, the pines bear a bumper crop of nuts. The nuts are a favorite food of the deer mouse. With a lot of food around, the number of deer mice rises. That's when the disease strikes, the Navajos said: when deer mice are plentiful.

The Navajo people knew the risk long before the CDC laboratories were ever built. Navajo tradition prohibits contact with mice. Navajos keep mice out of their homes and away from their food. Tribal custom dictates that clothes touched by mice be burned. Said a Navajo medicine woman, "The illness spreads in the air. In a closed room, the power of the mouse would take over and destroy you if it got in your eyes or nose or mouth." Cheek realized that the Navajo teachings were correct, but until 1993 no one had known why.

The Navajos also say that the disease will take the strongest and the healthiest. Again they were right. The hantavirus never appears in children under age 12. Scientists guess that an immature immune system may be the reason. Investigators find large, misshapen lymphocytes in the lungs, lymph nodes, and spleens of hantavirus victims. They guess that death comes not as a direct result of the virus but from the immune system's violent response to it. The leakage in the lungs may wash away the virus but kill the host in the process.

Today we know a lot about the hantavirus, but not enough. Although a test can diagnose it in its early stages, too many people show up with symptoms of what appears to be nothing more than a cold or flu, so they don't get tested. And although early treatment with antiviral drugs can save some, the course of the disease is perilous at best.

Furthermore, the hantavirus is not confined to the American Southwest. By 1995 similar hantaviruses had been found in 21 states and Canada, as well as in South America. The carrier is always a rodent but not always the deer mouse. Hantaviruses spread in the feces, urine, and saliva

of white-footed mice, cotton rats, and harvest mice, too.

The best treatment for hantavirus is prevention:

- Stay away from mice—indoors and out.
- Don't dig in the dirt where mice have been.
- Put garbage in mouse-proof bins.
- Don't handle mice. Use disposable traps or hire an exterminator.
- Keep weeds and high grass mowed near homes and buildings.
- When camping, don't sleep on bare ground.
- Don't leave food around the house or yard. It can attract mice.
- To clean sheds and garages, wear a mask and gloves. Spray the ground with bleach or Lysol® to kill the virus. Wait 15 minutes before sweeping. Wash body and clothes afterward.

All this trouble for a virus? Yes, and more, considering the official name given this killer in January 1994. It now bears the name of the area of the Navajo Nation where it was first isolated—Muerto Canyon, Valley of Death.

· · · · ·

CHAPTER FOUR

QUESTIONS
ABOUT ALLERGIES

*Allergy differs from most other diseases in that its victims . . .
seldom die and almost as seldom recover.*

• BERTON ROUECHÉ •

Is an Allergy an Immune Response?

Yes. The immune system makes a mistake. It can't tell "safe" from "harmful." Cat dander, ragweed pollen, and house dust pose no threat of disease. But in some people, the immune system gets it wrong and overreacts. T cells signal the production of IgE antibodies. IgE in the blood and lymph carries the allergen to mast cells in the skin and airways. The mast cells release histamine and other inflammatory chemicals.

These chemicals cause tiny blood vessels in the airways to stretch and leak. Fluid-soaked tissues swell. Smooth muscles contract. That makes breathing ragged. Histamine increases mucus production. It constricts breathing tubes. Eyes itch, turn red, and water. The nose gets stuffed or runny. The allergy sufferer sneezes, coughs, wheezes, gasps for breath. Histamine can also produce itchy, red, swollen skin, and rashes.

Some allergic responses occur rapidly, but some take hours, days, or weeks. IgE is not to blame for delayed responses. The attack of too many T cells on healthy tissue causes the trouble.

Yes, but the symptoms don't appear until the second time around. The first exposure sets the stage. The second starts the show.

Mast cells won't react to an allergen unless previously sensitized. That means they already have an IgE antibody specific to a particular allergen bound to them. For example, most people can breathe ragweed pollen all day and have no reaction. Only allergic people make IgE antibodies against ragweed pollen. These molecules bind to mast cells in the nose and air passages. They remain there after a first exposure. When ragweed pollen comes along again, the runny nose and itchy eyes of hay fever set in.

Breathing may be hazardous to your health. The most common allergens are inhaled from an environment full of antigens, typically:

- pollen: trees, grasses, weeds, or flowers;
- molds, also called mildew: the spores of fungi;
- pet dander: flakes of dog or cat skin, or their urine or saliva; rarely their fur (so short-haired pets aren't safe for allergy sufferers);
- house dust: especially house dust mites and fecal matter from mites and cockroaches in beds, drapes, and furniture.

Allergic reactions of the skin are common, too. Metal (especially nickel) in jewelry, poison ivy, poison oak, and some cosmetics can produce hives, redness, itching, or rashes.

While a tendency toward allergies is frequently inherited, inheriting a specific allergy is rare. Just because dad is allergic to shellfish doesn't mean that you will be.

What Is Hay Fever?

Hay fever isn't a fever and it has nothing to do with hay. (Just as rose fever isn't a fever and has nothing to do with roses.) Doctors call both hay fever and rose fever allergic rhinitis (rhinitis means a runny nose). It's an allergic reaction to plant materials in the air. Typically those are tree and grass pollens in the spring or ragweed pollen in late summer and early fall.

The cytokine interleukin-4 plays a role in initiating the allergic response. Eosinophils that migrate to the site release cytokines, including interleukins-4 and 5, that keep the inflammation going.

What's the Difference Between Hay Fever and Asthma?

Asthma has nothing to do with runny noses or watery eyes. Asthma is a tightening of the muscles around the bronchial tubes. The tightening—along with inflammation of the airway lining—causes the breathing tubes to narrow. Breathing becomes labored. Exhaling is especially difficult. One clue to asthma is a wheezing or whistling sound when breathing.

The pattern of an asthma attack varies from one person to another. Some people have sudden attacks, brought on by allergic reactions, respiratory infection, exercise, cold air, drugs, or food additives. Sometimes symptoms appear only at night or only in certain places, such as at school or at home. Emotions don't cause asthma, but they can trigger attacks or make symptoms worse.

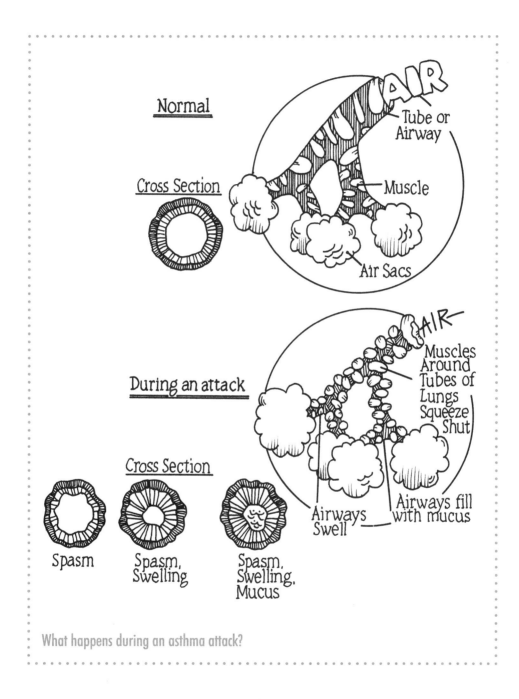

Normal

Cross Section

AIR

Tube or Airway

Muscle

Air Sacs

During an attack

AIR

Muscles Around Tubes of Lungs Squeeze Shut

Airways fill with mucus

Airways Swell

Cross Section

Spasm

Spasm, Swelling

Spasm, Swelling, Mucus

What happens during an asthma attack?

One reason for the confusion of hay fever with asthma is that some people have both. Allergies can provoke asthma attacks in susceptible individuals. For example, researchers in Chicago believe that cockroaches are the major cause of asthma among city children. Proteins in the droppings and carcasses of cockroaches are powerful antigens. The exhaust fumes from both diesel and gasoline engines are implicated, too. The main causes in the suburbs? Dust mites and cats.

Asthma and hay fever respond to different treatments. Drugs that block histamine help people with allergies. Decongestants open clogged airways for those with respiratory allergies. People who have asthma need medicines that expand and relax their bronchial tubes.

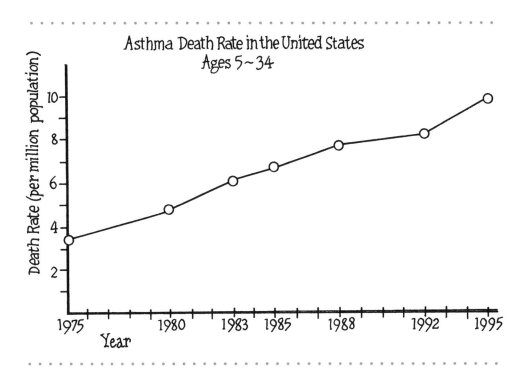

Asthma Death Rate in the United States
Ages 5~34

Is Breaking Out in Hives a Sign of an Allergy?

Roughly one in seven of us will break out in hives in any given year.[5] Is it an allergy? Maybe. Maybe not. Some 3,000 chemicals in the environment—both natural and human-made— cause skin outbreaks in sensitive individuals.[6]

In some people, the allergic nature of hives is obvious. They eat a certain food, and in only a few minutes their skin erupts in red welts. In such cases, the cause is the same as hay fever. IgE binds the allergen and attaches to mast cells in the skin. The mast cells release histamine. That triggers a release of fluids. The visible result is red, itchy, inflamed skin. Allergic hives can be brought on by drugs, cold, sun, infections, insect stings, alcohol, exercise, foods, hormones, or stress.

Hives don't always involve the immune system, however. Pressure on the skin, low temperatures, exercise, anxiety, tight clothing, or sunlight can bring on nonallergic hives. Usually, it's hard to tell whether an immune response is occurring. The cause of hives remains a mystery. About 70 percent of the time, the welts go away on their own, without treatment.[7] Severe, persistent, or recurring cases may require a doctor's care.

Are Allergies Imaginary? Is Asthma an Emotional Disorder?

Allergies are an inappropriate reaction of the immune system. Asthma is a constriction of the bronchial tubes. They aren't imaginary, and people don't "make them up." Stress and emotional factors can trigger allergic attacks or make symptoms worse. But allergies aren't the hallmark of hypochondria that some people believe them to be.

How Do Skin Tests Diagnose Allergies?

When allergens overstimulate the immune system, IgE antibodies against that allergen form and circulate in the blood. Allergy skin tests work because the allergen applied to the skin binds with IgE and produces a visible response.

To test for a particular allergy, a doctor applies a drop of a suspected allergen to the skin. Tiny scratches or pinpricks let the substance penetrate the skin's outer layers. After about 20 minutes, the skin's response tells the tale. A red spot that looks like a mosquito bite signals the possibility of an allergy. Additional tests may confirm the diagnosis.

Can Allergies Kill?

Yes. Anaphylactic shock is a sudden, extreme allergic reaction. It involves the entire body, not just the skin or airways. Blood pressure plummets. The person becomes dizzy and may lose consciousness. Severe anaphylactic shock can stop the heart. Although such a severe allergic reaction is rare, its causes are not. Horse serum (in which some vaccines are prepared), penicillin (a commonly prescribed antibiotic), nuts, shellfish, strawberries, and other foods and drugs cause anaphylactic shock in certain individuals.

Another fairly common cause is an insect sting. Any sting will produce some swelling, pain, and redness at the site. The allergic response is far more severe and widespread. Itching and swelling occur on all the skin. The tongue may swell, and the voice may become hoarse. The chest feels tight, and breathing is difficult. People who know they are allergic to insect stings often carry kits that include a dose of adrenaline to counteract such symptoms. Prompt attention from a physician is essential.

Are Some People Allergic to Drugs and Medicines?

Yes, but rarely. The most common drug allergy is penicillin. About 5 people in 100 are allergic to penicillin. That antibiotic accounts for some 90 percent of all drug allergies.[8] Chances run between 1 and 3 percent for most other drugs. Aspirin, some anesthetics, opiate drugs such as codeine, heparin (an anticlot drug for blood), sulfa drugs, and such antibiotics as streptomycin can also trigger allergic responses. Only one in every 10,000 allergic reactions to drugs results in death.[9]

Don't confuse drug allergies with side effects. If a drug causes drowsiness, dry mouth, or stomach cramps, safe use may be possible. In those cases, the drug itself—not the immune system—is the threat. Overdoses of any drug can be dangerous, even deadly, whether the immune system is involved or not.

Drug allergies usually develop after a period of sensitization. Take the drug once, and all is well. But the second use brings on a rash, shortness of breath, shock, or kidney failure. Drug allergies seldom strike infants or the elderly. The immaturity or inadequacy of their immune systems reduces their risk.

How Are Allergies Treated?

The best way to escape allergy is to avoid the allergen, but that's not always easy. Pollen is difficult to escape, even indoors, though closed windows, air conditioners, and air filters can help. Clean bed linens, new furniture and mattresses, and antiallergenic mattress covers can diminish dust-mite allergies. So can regular vacuuming and dehumidifiers that keep air so dry that mites can't flourish. Bathing cats and dogs doesn't prevent allergies to animal dander, nor have dander-free pets yet been bred. If you are allergic to cats and dogs, consider fish or reptiles as pets.

Over-the-counter and prescription medicines can relieve some symptoms. Antihistamines reduce sneezing, sniffling, and itching. Decongestants decrease blood supply to the nasal membranes, causing them to shrink. Side effects may include insomnia and irritability. Doctors don't recommend decongestant nasal sprays for allergies. They can produce a "rebound effect." Stopping their use causes nasal membranes to swell again. Symptoms return or worsen. Sometimes, doctors prescribe corticosteroid sprays or sprays containing cromolyn sodium to help clear a stuffy nose or control sneezing and itching.

How Do Allergy Shots Work?

Antiallergy shots or vaccinations are also called immunotherapy. The treatment involves injecting small amounts of allergen under the skin. The injections must be repeated in increasing doses every three to eight days for several months, then every two weeks to four weeks for several years. The doctor watches for side effects ranging from irritation at the site of the shot to more serious reactions such as tight throat and shortness of breath. If the shots work, the immune response gradually decreases.

This process is called desensitization. No one is quite sure why it works. Some experts think that desensitization causes less IgE to be produced and less histamine to be released. Others think that the increasing doses cause B cells to make IgG. IgG molecules are faster and smaller than IgE. Perhaps they reach the allergen and destroy it before IgE can trigger the release of histamine.

"Allergy vaccinations are like all vaccinations—they improve the natural defenses of the immune system," says Dr. Ira Finegold, past president of the American College of Allergy, Asthma, and Immunology. "In the hands of a well-trained and experienced health professional, allergy vaccinations are very safe and highly effective," he adds.[10] A lot of people agree. More than a million Americans have taken allergy injections since immunotherapy first began in the 1940s.[11]

The Fracas Over Food Allergies

. . . . .

There is no sincerer love than the love of food.

GEORGE BERNARD SHAW

. . . . .

Consider these two scenes:

Scene 1: Gasping and wheezing, Bobby Kendall, age 4, is wheeled into the emergency room. His worried parents hover nearby, teary-eyed and red-faced. "We've been so careful," his mother whimpers. "No peanut brittle, no peanut butter sandwiches. All our friends know that Bobby can't have peanuts. How could this have happened?"

Scene 2: Miriam Carpenter, age 40, munches an enzyme tablet before dashing off to a birthday party. "I'm allergic to dairy foods," Miriam tells a friend. "It's not the only food I'm allergic to," she reveals. "Cucumbers give me stomach cramps and gas, too."

Pretend you are a doctor. Can you diagnose Bobby and Miriam from the following list?

- Food poisoning: Illness caused by consuming food contaminated with poisonous substances, disease-causing microbes, or parasites.
- Food allergy: An overreaction of the immune system to a chemical constituent (usually a protein) in a food.
- Food intolerance: An uncomfortable or abnormal response of the

gastrointestinal tract to a food or food additive.

- Pharmacological food reaction: A response to a druglike substance contained in foods (for example, coffee "jitters" from caffeine).
- Food anaphylaxis: An allergic reaction so severe as to be life-threatening.

Score a point if you decided that Miriam's symptoms result from a food intolerance not involving the immune system. If you guessed that Bobby has a food allergy so severe it has brought on anaphylaxis, give yourself another point.

Bobby knew he shouldn't eat peanuts. So did his friends and family. But peanuts come in many forms. The fast food restaurant where Bobby had eaten safely many times in the past changed brands of cooking oil. The new brand contained peanut oil. Bobby had a few French fries. The tiny amount of peanut oil they contained sent Bobby into anaphylactic shock.

True food allergies like Bobby's are rare. In most people, the stomach and intestines are about 98 percent effective in preventing complete proteins from entering the blood.[12]

Digestion breaks proteins into safe amino acids. Even the few protein molecules that do cross the wall of the digestive system into the blood seldom cause trouble.

Still, in individuals like Bobby, the immune system can mistake the food protein for an invading microorganism. The body's immune system swings into high gear, producing IgE. The IgE attaches to mast cells. Mast cells release irritating chemicals that cause blood vessels to widen and leak. Smooth muscles contract. In the digestive tract that causes vomiting, stomach pains, and diarrhea. Swelling of airways, wheezing, and difficulty breathing can follow. About 50 Americans die each year from anaphylactic reactions to food.[13]

Miriam is not allergic to dairy products. No immune response is involved. She gets a tummy ache when she eats ice cream because she lacks the enzyme lactase. Without it, she cannot digest lactose, a sugar found in uncultured milk products. What she can't use as food, the bacteria in her digestive tract can. Their action gives Miriam gas and diarrhea. Miriam has the cause wrong but the treatment right.

Lactase tablets provide the enzyme her body is missing and let her eat ice cream comfortably.

While many of us believe we are allergic to a food, only 5 percent of children under three and fewer than 2 percent of adults actually are. That's about 4 million Americans.[14] That number is small compared with the nearly 60 million residents of the United States who cope with hay fever, asthma, and skin allergies.[15] People who think they are allergic to many foods are usually wrong. No scientific evidence supports the belief that food allergies cause fatigue, poor memory, or lack of concentration. Scientific studies don't confirm what many parents believe: that sugar makes children misbehave.

Unscrupulous or misguided individuals and companies steal millions from gullible consumers with bogus food allergy tests and treatments. The National Council on Health Fraud warns that some advertised tests for food allergy are unreliable, including:

- hair analysis,
- applied kinesiology (measuring muscle strength while holding a container of food),
- radionics (electronic devices that claim to measure energy produced by allergenic foods), and
- dowsing (diagnosing food allergies with a dowsing rod or pendulum).

The National Institutes of Health warn consumers to avoid so-called cytotoxicity testing, in which a technician looks through a microscope to see if white cells die in the presence of a food. Also unreliable are injections under the tongue or skin that claim to link food allergies to arthritis. The immune complex assay said to reveal antibodies bound to food allergens in the blood is useless, too. Everyone has such complexes, whether allergic or not.

A true food allergy is best diagnosed by a qualified physician. The diagnosis requires a medical history, physical exam, and tests of immune function. A suspected allergy can be confirmed by avoiding a food for several weeks, then trying it again while monitoring symptoms. The best way to treat food allergies is to eliminate the offending food from the diet for a while. A food allergy often goes away on its own after a few years of avoidance.

• • • • •

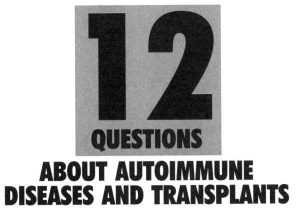

CHAPTER FIVE

12 QUESTIONS

ABOUT AUTOIMMUNE
DISEASES AND TRANSPLANTS

"Humans get no warranty when they are born. There are no recalls, no free replacements of parts if we come off the biological assembly line with a missing or faulty element of the immunological apparatus."

• ROBERT S. DESOWITZ •

What Is an Autoimmune Disease?

Sometimes the immune system gets it wrong. It attacks the cells of healthy tissues and organs. Such disorders are called autoimmune (meaning self-immune). No one knows why the immune system suddenly confuses "self" and "not self," but the outcomes can be life threatening.

Autoimmune diseases can occur at any place in the body. The symptoms depend on the site. An attack on the joints is rheumatoid arthritis. Destruction of the insulin-producing cells of the pancreas is diabetes mellitus. An immune attack on the thyroid gland results in Hashimoto disease (too little thyroid hormone) or Graves' disease (too much).

When the immune system runs amok, it can hurt the body in any or all of three ways:

- a direct attack on an organ;
- a by-product of action elsewhere;
- a response that starts at one place and spreads to another.

The kidney offers examples of all three. Goodpasture syndrome is a direct attack of antibodies on the membranes of the kidney. It usually starts after exposure to some poisonous chemical. Another autoimmune disease, SLE (systemic lupus erythematosus), causes kidney damage indirectly. Clumps of antigen bound to antibody circulate in the blood. They lodge in the kidneys and damage them. The disorder called Wegener granulomatosis is an example of a response that spreads. The immune attack starts in the airways. It moves to the kidneys later.

How Can the Immune System Make Mistakes?

Several ways are possible:
- *Inventory*. Early in life, the thymus gland takes stock of the proteins that are "self." The information is stored much like an inventory. If a protein is accidentally left out of the inventory, the immune system may later fail to recognize it as "self."
- *Late Additions*: As a person grows older, new tissues develop that the immune system did not inventory in childhood. An example is sperm cells in a male, not produced until puberty. If the immune system cannot recognize the sperm as simply another form of "self," it will destroy sperm cells and cause sterility.
- *Exposure*: Proteins that were hidden from the immune system can be exposed by accident. For example, an eye injury can lead to the formation of antibodies that attack the eye, causing blindness. An-

other example is heart surgery. It can spur the immune system to produce antibodies that attack the heart muscle.

- *Mutation*: Radiation, a drug, or a virus can cause a mutation (change in DNA, the genetic material). Or sometimes mutation simply happens at random or by chance. Whatever the reason for it, mutation leads to a change in a protein. The immune system recognizes the changed protein as foreign and attacks. It destroys not only the protein but also the entire cell along with it.

- *Imitation*: Some pathogens carry proteins that resemble normal body proteins. In attacking the pathogen, the immune system also attacks body cells. Chagas' disease is an example. A parasite carries the same antigen as heart muscle and nerve cells. The immune system destroys all three.

- *Deregulation*: Anything that disrupts the balance among T cells, B cells, and antibodies can spell trouble. Too many helper T cells or too few suppressors can push antibody manufacture out of control. The surplus of antibodies then damages healthy tissue.

What Is Lupus and How Is It Treated?

The name lupus comes from the Latin word for wolf. Early observers thought the butterfly rash that spreads across the nose and cheekbones of people with this disease looked like a wolf or the bite of a wolf. Doctors today recognize three forms of lupus. One is limited to the skin. Drugs induce another. Most of the time, lupus is used as a shorthand word for a third form: systemic lupus erythematosus (SLE). SLE is more serious and long-lasting than the other two forms.

SLE is an attack of the immune system on skin, joints, blood vessels, kidneys, and sometimes the heart. The body mistakenly manufactures antibodies that destroy its own DNA. Symptoms include achy or swollen joints, fatigue, fevers, and skin rashes.

The Lupus Foundation reports that more people have lupus than AIDS, cerebral palsy, multiple sclerosis, sickle-cell anemia, and cystic fibrosis combined. That totals perhaps 2 million Americans. Nine out of ten are women.[1] Although SLE is mild for most, it can prove life threatening for some.

The cause of SLE is unknown. It runs in families, so genes may be involved. The environment plays a part, too. SLE often begins after an infection. Antibiotics, ultraviolet light, stress, or pregnancy can also bring on the disorder. Hormones may explain why women get the disease more often than men do.

Doctors cannot cure SLE, but they can often manage its symptoms. Exercise improves flexibility in stiff joints and sore muscles. Aspirin, acetaminophen (such as Tylenol®), and anti-inflammatory drugs ease pain. Immune-suppressing drugs can dampen attacks. SLE patients can learn to help themselves. Sometimes staying out of the sun or stopping the use of certain drugs helps.

What Is Arthritis and How Is It Treated?

Arthritis is swelling, pain, and stiffening of the joints. The most common form is osteoarthritis. It comes with age. It results from years of wear and tear. It's not an autoimmune disease.

Rheumatoid arthritis, on the other hand, is autoimmune. Its pain results from an attack of white blood cells on the synovium, a membrane that lines the joints. Inflammatory chemicals cause the synovium to thicken. They digest cartilage, bones, tendons, and ligaments in the joint, robbing it of its strength and flexibility.

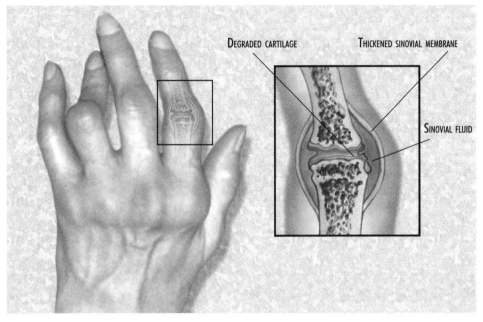

Note the changes in the joint caused by rheumatoid arthritis.

In the United States alone, 2.5 million people suffer from rheumatoid arthritis. Three out of four are women.[2] The disease generally begins between the ages of twenty and fifty, but it can strike at any age. Nearly 300,000 Americans under the age of sixteen have juvenile rheumatoid arthritis.[3]

No one knows what causes the immune system to attack the joints. The disease runs in families, but the patterns of inheritance are unclear. Some people with the disease have a protein in their blood called rheumatoid factor, but not everyone who has the protein gets arthritis. A virus may have something to do with it. An infection can provoke a first attack in susceptible people.

In the past, rheumatoid arthritis sentenced many people to wheel-chairs. Today treatment helps many lead active lives. Aspirin or other over-the-counter pain relievers are enough for some. Drugs that suppress the immune response and medicines that reduce inflammation help others. Sometimes surgeons tighten or loosen tendons, fuse bones, or implant plastic or metal joints. Rest, exercise, and a healthy diet also help.

Drugs used against the parasitic disease malaria can halt rheumatoid arthritis in some patients. How? Ronald Macfarlane at the University of Iowa thinks he knows the answer. When fighting a bacterial infection, immune cells engulf and digest invaders. They also release some bacterial DNA, which activates an immune response. Macfarlane thinks that antimalarial drugs block the activation.

What Is Diabetes and How Is It Treated?

Not all forms of diabetes are autoimmune, but Type I diabetes probably is. Type I is also called juvenile diabetes because it begins in young people. It is an attack of the immune system on the insulin-producing cells of the pancreas. As a result, the body cannot make insulin. Insulin is the hormone in the blood that helps body cells break down glucose. The chemical breakdown of that simple sugar releases the energy stored in the molecule. Without insulin, body cells starve.

According to the Juvenile Diabetes Foundation, 16 million Americans have diabetes in some form. The disease kills one American every three minutes. It reduces life expectancy by as much as one-third.[4]

Diabetics take insulin injections or tablets to keep blood insulin sugar normal. Someday, transplants of insulin-producing cells may cure diabetes. Many scientific problems must be solved first. Researchers at

Harvard hope to transplant insulin-making cells without sentencing patients to years of immune-suppressing drugs. They are looking for ways to trick the immune system into accepting transplants. They must also stop the attack process, or the transplanted cells will die just as the body's own cells did.

Do Any Autoimmune Diseases Affect the Skin?

Yes. The term pemphigus refers to a group of skin diseases that involve the immune system. Normally, cells in the outer layer of healthy skin produce a protein called keratin. Keratin makes skin, hair, and fingernails strong. People with pemphigus make IgG antibodies against their own keratin-producing cells. The cells detach from the skin and form painful blisters.

Psoriasis is another autoimmune skin disease. The skin grows to five or ten times its normal thickness.[5] Although killer T cells occur normally in skin, their numbers grow far larger in the skin of people with psoriasis. In 1995, James Krueger at Rockefeller University gave patients with severe psoriasis a form of interleukin-2 that destroys killer T cells. Their rough, scaly skin lesions disappeared. Krueger calls psoriasis the most common human autoimmune disease.[6] More than 6 million Americans have it.[7]

What Is Multiple Sclerosis (MS) and How Is It Treated?

In people with MS, T cells cause inflammation of the brain and spinal cord. The immune system attacks the myelin sheath that surrounds nerve cells. "The myelin acts as an insulator of the electrical impulses that travel through the nervous system, delivering messages to and from the brain. If you damage the myelin, you short out the nerve," explains Garry Fathman of Stanford University.[8]

Worldwide, more than a million people have MS, an estimated 400,000 in the United States alone.[9] Two-thirds are women, usually first stricken in their 20s or 30s. Symptoms include double vision, weakness, lack of coordination and balance, fatigue, and paralysis. No one knows what starts MS. Hormonal factors, virus infections, and an inherited susceptibility all seem to play a part.

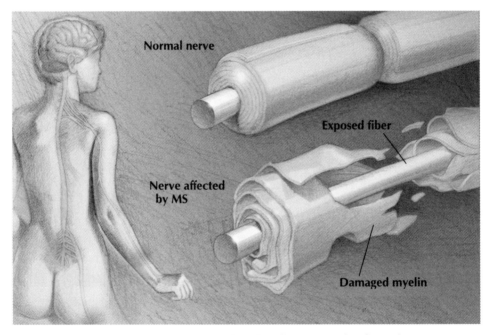

Normal nerve

Exposed fiber

Nerve affected by MS

Damaged myelin

Multiple sclerosis gets its name from areas of hardened scar tissue that form along nerve fibers. When nerve impulses reach damaged areas, they are delayed or blocked.

MS can't be cured, but its symptoms can be treated and its progression slowed. Steroid drugs reduce inflammation of nerve tissue. Interferons dampen the immune attack. Other drugs alleviate muscle spasms and control pain.

Many MS research projects are investigating antiviral drugs, vaccines, and vitamin therapy. In lab animals, U.S. and German scientists have transplanted myelin-making cells from a healthy donor. A team at Stanford is studying a cytokine, interleukin-4, as a way of turning down the immune response. If it works, their procedure could help people with rheumatoid arthritis and diabetes as well as MS.

Can Transplants Help People With Autoimmune Diseases?

Sometimes. In 1998, twenty-four-year-old Kirstin Wallin became the third person in the United States to receive a stem-cell transplant. (Stem cells in bone marrow manufacture blood cells.)

Kirstin had a serious autoimmune disease called scleroderma. The disease hardens and stretches the skin. That leads to splitting and open sores. Joints lock. Hands become set in a clawlike position. Scleroderma can clench the jaw so tight that eating is difficult. In severe cases such as Kirstin's, chances of surviving five years with scleroderma are only 50:50. From 150,000 to 500,000 Americans have scleroderma. Four out of five of them are women.[10]

Scleroderma comes from an overproduction of the connective tissue called collagen. Too much collagen damages skin, heart, lungs, and kidneys. No one yet knows how or why the immune system speeds up collagen production. One cytokine, transforming growth factor beta or TGFb, causes certain cells in the deeper layer of skin to increase in number. TGFb occurs in high concentrations in the skin of people with scleroderma. How that fact relates to the disease remains a mystery.

Whatever the means, the transplant worked for Kirstin. An Oregon newspaper told her story under the headline "Experimental Treatment Restores Woman's Youth." The headline was an exaggeration, but the story was no less miraculous. The transplant of stem cells halted the autoimmune attack. "I feel like I'm fifteen again," Kirstin said.[11]

Why Do Women Get Autoimmune Diseases More Often Than Men Do?

No one knows for sure, but hormones seem to be an obvious answer. Men and women make the same sex hormones. The only difference is in amounts. In women, the levels of female hormones, estrogen and progesterone, are high. Relatively small amounts of male hormones circulate in their blood. In men, of course, the opposite holds true.

Female hormones may be beneficial most of the time. Among healthy people, women generally have stronger immune systems than men do. They have higher levels of IgG and IgM in their blood. Their immune systems generally react more strongly against pathogens. They resist infections better.

A great strength can also be a great weakness. Women's hormonal levels vary at different times in life, particularly at adolescence, during pregnancy, and after bearing a child. Childbirth seems to trigger a number of autoimmune diseases in women, which hints that hormones cause some immune change. Birth-control pills containing high levels of estrogen have brought on rheumatoid arthritis in a few women. Some research shows high levels of estrogen in both men and women with SLE. In animals, treatment with male hormones seems to slow lupus in females. (That's a treatment most women would not want.)

The immune system destroys any foreign protein. This self-defense is beneficial most of the time, but it can work against medical science. Doctors can save lives by transplanting organs. But for a transplant to succeed, the immune response must be blocked. Early attempts at organ transplants failed. The surgery was successful, but the immune system destroyed the transplanted organ. Organ rejection is a form of cell-mediated immunity. Helper T cells detect proteins on the surface of the transplanted tissue as foreign. Killer T cells destroy proteins, cells, and all.

Drugs that suppress the immune system prevent rejection. The drugs have drawbacks, however. Transplant patients must take them for long periods of time, sometimes for the rest of their lives. The drugs depress the entire immune system. Transplant patients live in fear of infectious diseases.

Researchers want to find alternatives to immune-suppressing drugs. Scientists at Research Corporation Technologies in Arizona found an antibody that seems to interrupt the immune response without killing all T cells. Researchers at the University of Pittsburgh use genetically altered immune cells to disable the T cell response. Cancer researchers in Boston have used interleukin-11 to block rejection of bone marrow transplants.

What Is Tissue Typing and Why Is It Done?

Tissue typing is also called histocompatibility testing. This laboratory test identifies the antigens present on the surface of cells. These antigens serve as markers. The immune system distinguishes "self" and "not self" by "inspecting" them. Each person has a unique combination of histocompatibility antigens. The more nearly alike the antigens of donor and recipient, the greater the chance of a successful transplant. That's why identical twins, siblings, or close relatives are usually better-matched donors than strangers.

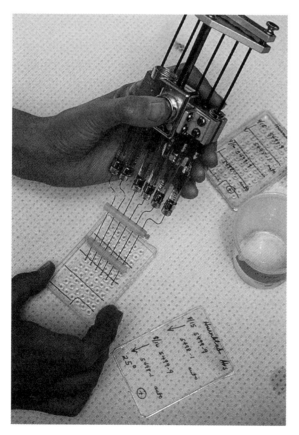

A lab technician tests small patches of tissue to determine suitability for organ transplants.

Why Doesn't a Pregnant Woman's Body Reject Her Fetus?

That question has puzzled experts for at least a century. No one as yet has come up with a good answer.

To the immune system, the fetus is a lot of foreign protein. Half of its genetic material comes from the mother. That's "self." But the other half comes from the father, which the mother's body recognizes as "not self." Often, the mother and the fetus don't even share the same blood type. Any transplant from an infant to its mother—for example, a skin graft—would be immediately rejected. Yet the mother's body tolerates—even nourishes—a composite of foreign antigens that can grow to 10 pounds (4.5 kilograms) or more before birth.

One thing is clear. The uterus must have some way of blocking rejection. The placenta must surely be involved in some way. Does it produce chemicals that stop the mother's immune cells? Does it manufacture immune-suppressing substances? No one knows, but the acceptance of this antigenic stranger is not a temporary thing. Fetal cells persist in a mother's blood long after her child has grown into adulthood.

Pumps, Pigs, and Primates

· · · · ·

Life has always been dangerous. We can only make life better by pressing on, applying our best scientific research and our best judgment.

FREDERICK A. MURPHY
(CENTERS FOR DISEASE CONTROL AND PREVENTION)

Does it make sense to pursue risky research that could cost millions of lives in order to pursue something that may or may not be successful?

PEGGY L. CARLSON
(HUMANE SOCIETY OF AMERICA)

· · · · ·

In 1967, Louis Washkansky, a South African dentist, turned fiction to fact. Washkansky, received the first successful heart transplant. He lived 18 days before his body rejected his donated pump.

Three decades later, Tony Johnson changed history for a different reason. The engineer from Taunton, Massachusetts, received the world's first successful xenograft of brain cells.

A xenograft is a transplant of tissue from one species to another. Johnson's surgeons transplanted not an entire organ but only a few brain cells. The cells came from a fetal pig. The pig's cells made a brain chemical called dopamine, which Johnson's brain could not. Before the transplant, Johnson was confined to a wheelchair. He could neither talk nor feed himself. After the operation, he ate, spoke, and played golf.

As promising as such experiments may seem, they're a long way from xenotransplants—putting whole organs from nonhumans into humans. But some say there's good reason to try. First, the demand for human-donated organs always exceeds the supply. Annually, more than 40,000 patients wait for kidneys, hearts, or lungs. Nine people die every day waiting for an organ.[12]

Another problem is rejection. Transplant recipients must take immune-suppressing drugs for months or years. Blocking their immunity makes patients susceptible to infections, some of which can kill. Xenotransplants might solve both of these problems if (1) a large supply of organs could be "farmed" in animals such as pigs; and (2) the organs could be genetically engineered to prevent rejection.

Xenotransplantation is not a new idea. In 1906, French surgeon Mathieu Jaboulay transplanted a pig's kidney into one human patient and a goat's liver into another.[13] Given the knowledge of immunity available at that time, it's no surprise that both patients died. In 1964, Thomas Starzl at the University of Pittsburgh failed in an attempt to transplant a baboon's kidney to a human. His patient died from infections accompanied by kidney failure. That same year, a chimpanzee-to-human transplant fared a little better. The patient lived for nine months before the kidney failed.

In 1984 the child the newspapers called "Baby Fae" was born prematurely with a severely malformed heart. She could not live long without a transplant. Because no human heart small enough for Baby Fae was available, surgeons at Loma Linda University in California attempted a xenotransplant. They gave Baby Fae the heart of a baboon. The operation went well, but Fae died of organ rejection and infection after the operation.

In 1992 two other transplants from baboons were tried—this time of livers. The livers functioned well, but the patients died from infections. That same year, two women received livers from pigs. The transplants were not meant to be permanent. They were intended as "bridges" to tide the patients over until human donors were found. In both women the livers functioned well, but one of the patients died before a human organ could be found.

The experiments provoked objections from supporters of animal rights. Primates, such as baboons and chimpanzees, are humankind's closest relatives. It's wrong to sacrifice them to our own needs, some argue.

One answer to such objections is to use animals that are routinely raised and slaughtered for food. Pigs are easy to breed and produce large litters. Their size and weight are similar to those of humans. Pigs are easy to care for. Few people object to killing pigs.

The human immune system should reject pig organs just as it does human ones, so what's the advantage? The answer lies in genetic engineering. If pig cells can be induced to display human antigens on their surfaces, then the body will accept the transplanted organ as "self."

Here's how it's done. First, researchers remove a fertilized egg from the uterus of a female pig. Next, they insert human antigen-coding genes into the fertilized egg. Finally, they return the egg to the mother's womb and let the embryo develop normally. If the gene transplant works, the baby pig's cells will manufacture human proteins.

If xenotransplants are so promising, why aren't they being tried often? Scientists and political leaders fear introducing some new infectious disease into the human population. A virus might lie dormant in pig cells, only transforming into a lethal pathogen in the human body. Or the immune-suppressing drugs that transplant patients take might prompt a virus to grow and adapt. Once imported into human beings in a xenotransplant, the pathogen might spread as others do—through blood, air, water, or food.

The transfer of a disease from nonhumans to humans happens in nature. For example, the Hong Kong flu virus lay harmlessly in waterbirds for many years. Then it struck chickens and caused massive kills on poultry farms. Now it infects people. How it migrated to humans remains unknown. Diseases can be minor in animals but major in humans. For instance, the herpes virus B gives monkeys mild cold sores but causes fatal encephalitis in people.

Animals used for xenotransplant organs could not be raised under ordinary farming conditions. The possibility of infection would be too great. The animals would need to be raised in germ-free medical facilities. Such organ farming raises ethical questions. Is it cruel to raise young pigs in sterile isolation? Have we the right to impose stresses upon other animal species that we ourselves could not tolerate? Can human beings in good conscience use other species for such selfish (some say gruesome) purposes?

A 1998 survey sponsored by the National Kidney Foundation revealed that 94 percent of Americans know about the shortage of donor organs. Nearly two-thirds regard xenotransplantation as an acceptable option. Nearly three in every four of us would consider a xenotransplant for a loved one if no suitable human organ could be found.[14] Not all objections have vanished, however. One-third of respondents to a Research!America survey thought research on xenotransplants should end.[15]

. . . . .

CHAPTER SIX

15
QUESTIONS
ABOUT VACCINES

A gram of prevention is worth a kilo of cure.
• TRADITIONAL MAXIM, UPDATED •

How Were
Vaccines First
Developed?

A vaccine is a human-made substance that pro-vides immune benefits without causing the dis-ease. Doctors saw the value in vaccinating people long before they understood what the vaccine might actually be doing.

In 1796, English physician Edward Jenner scratched material from a cowpox sore into the arm of James Phipps, a healthy eight-year-old boy. Jenner had noticed that milkmaids seldom got smallpox. They did, however, catch cowpox—a relatively mild disease—from the cattle they tended. Jenner thought that giving James cowpox might protect the boy from smallpox—just as the milkmaids were protected.

James got cowpox and recovered. Two months later Jenner scratched the material from a smallpox sore into the boy's arm. (Such an experiment would be illegal today.) James stayed healthy. The vaccine (its name is derived from *vacca*, the Latin word for cow) had succeeded.

Jenner never knew why his vaccine worked. No one of his time knew anything about immunity. It wasn't even known that microbes cause many diseases. At first, the medical community resisted Jenner's ideas. After another doctor tried Jenner's experiment with the same results, people started to believe. The royal families of Europe eagerly sought vaccination to escape the scourge of smallpox.

Nearly a century later, the French biochemist Louis Pasteur tried another kind of vaccine. Pasteur injected a boy who had been bitten by a rabid dog. The injection was serum from the blood of a rabbit that had died from rabies. The boy did not get rabies.

Pasteur had the wrong idea about why his vaccine worked. He thought it used up all the food that disease-causing organisms needed to grow. He was soon proved wrong. The German scientist Emil von Behring worked with diphtheria. He and another German, Paul Ehrlich, defined the term "antibody." They showed that Pasteur's first rabies vaccine transferred antibodies from a rabbit to a human. Von Behring developed an antitoxin (poison blocker) against diphtheria. He and Ehrlich also established the lock-and-key hypothesis of how an antibody works.

Early in the twentieth century, researchers developed vaccines against typhoid fever, whooping cough, and tetanus. In the 1950s and 1960s, vaccines to protect against polio and measles were added to the list. Today most children receive these vaccines early in life.

How Do
Vaccines
Work?

A lot of "information gathering" must take place before plasma cells can produce antibodies. When a pathogen enters the body, antigen-presenting cells ingest some of the invaders. They then attach some of the invader's foreign proteins to their MHC docks. Helper T cells inspect those docks. When they find a foreign protein, they signal B cells to produce antibodies. All this preparation takes time. In a person who had had the disease or a vaccine, the preparation is finished ahead of time. Having a disease gives the immune system the information it needs to produce and store memory cells. So do vaccines. Memory cells stored in the lymph nodes make the quick response possible.

Some vaccines use live, but weakened, pathogens. Live vaccines don't produce the disease, but they do evoke a strong antibody response. Another kind of vaccine uses dead pathogens. The proteins from the viral coat or bacterial membrane may be all that is needed to initiate the formation of antibodies and the storage of memory cells.

What Kinds of Vaccines Do We Use Today?

Before the 1990s vaccines were always one of three types:

Type	Limitations	Examples
Killed bacteria or viruses	The immune system's response to dead pathogens is often weak, meaning that booster shots are needed.	influenza, cholera, bubonic plague, hepatitis A
Live but weakened (attenuated) bacteria or viruses	Live vaccines risk (very rarely) producing the disease.	measles, mumps, rubella
Toxoids (inactivated toxins)	Toxoids are effective only against those diseases caused not by a pathogen itself but by a poison it produces.	tetanus, diphtheria

Both of the first two types are used to prevent polio. In 1954 children received Jonas Salk's first vaccine against polio. It used dead polioviruses. It produced a weak immune response and required booster shots. In 1961, Albert Sabin's live-but-weakened polio vaccine became available. It promised strong, lifetime immunity against a crippling disease that had terrified parents.

New kinds of vaccines have been developed. They include:

- Conjugate Vaccines: Some bacteria "wear coats." Their outer capsules hide their antigens from the immune system. Conjugate vaccines hook an antigen that the immune system can recognize to the capsule. The vaccine that prevents one kind of flu is a conjugate vaccine.

Polio pioneers: Children who took part in the early trials of the Salk polio vaccine

- Subunit Vaccines: It doesn't take a whole organism to start an immune response. A small part of a pathogen can sometimes do the job. Subunit vaccines protect against particular forms of pneumonia and meningitis.

Are Vaccination and Immunization the Same Thing?

No. Vaccination is the process of giving a vaccine. Immunization is the process of acquiring immunity. Vaccination may or may not bring about immunization. Immunization may be acquired naturally, without a vaccine.

Will Any New Vaccines be Used in the Future?

Maybe. In 1997 researchers were hard at work on vaccines to fight more than 75 infectious diseases.[1]

Future vaccines may not use whole organisms, either living or dead. More likely, they'll rely on a protein from a pathogen to prime the immune system. Recombinant DNA techniques let laboratories manufacture pathogen proteins safely and cheaply. First a bit of genetic material (DNA or RNA) is taken from a pathogen. It is then merged or transplanted into a harmless strain of bacteria. The transplanted genes cause the bacteria to make a protein that the pathogen makes. In cell culture, the bacteria multiply. They make the protein in large quantities. The protein can then be extracted from the culture and used to make a vaccine. If all goes well, the protein will activate antibody production, just as the whole, live pathogen would.

Another new approach is the recombinant vector vaccine. A vector is a weakened virus that can accept DNA or RNA from a pathogen. When the vector enters the blood, it should provoke an immune response against the material it carries. This approach might work against AIDS or hepatitis B. Safety and effectiveness must first be tested.

Research on "naked DNA" vaccines excites many scientists. The idea is similar to the vector vaccine, but no vector is needed. Some DNA from a pathogen is injected into muscle. There, it causes a foreign protein to be produced. The protein should stimulate the immune system to make antibodies against it. If the whole pathogen ever shows up, the body will be ready to mount a strong response. If the DNA continues to control manufacture of the protein for many years, such immunity could last a lifetime. No boosters needed!

Are Vaccines Always Shots?

No, and maybe tomorrow's kids may *never* need to face needles and syringes. Researchers are developing ways to give vaccines through the membranes of the mouth, nose, and throat. Some tests of a flu vaccine delivered in a nasal spray were successful in St. Louis. The vaccine prevented influenza and reduced the number of ear infections in children.

Imagine getting vaccinated from the fruits and vegetables on your dinner plate! A team at Cornell University transplanted genes from bacteria to potato plants. The potatoes grew and made a bacterial protein. Volunteers who ate the potatoes produced antibodies against the protein. The antibodies showed up in their blood. The World Health Organization reports that more than 2 million children die each year of diseases that could be prevented.[2] Inexpensive and easy-to-distribute edible vaccines could save many lives, especially in nations where medical facilities and supplies are limited.

A scientist at Cornell University with vaccine-producing potato plants

Which Is Better, Developing My Own Immunity or Borrowing Someone Else's?

Your own is stronger and lasts longer, but borrowing from another person or a nonhuman animal can save your life in an emergency.

There are two kinds of immunization. In active immunization, the vaccine or disease "teaches" the immune system to recognize a poison, virus, or bacterium. Vaccines that use live or weakened pathogens induce active immunity. The outcome is the same as having the disease and recovering from it. Active immunization can last a lifetime.

Passive immunity results when antibodies from one person or animal are transferred to another. Antibodies (IgG) and antitoxins give short-term protection. This "borrowed" immunity lasts only a few weeks or months, but that period of time may be all that is needed to save a life. Doctors use three substances to give passive immunity:

- Standard human immune globulin is concentrated from human blood serum. It's mostly IgG. People who want to travel to certain countries can get short-term protection against hepatitis A this way.
- Specific human immune globulin is antibodies against a particular disease in concentrated form. One such preparation may be given to newborns of mothers who have hepatitis B.
- Antibodies from animal serum (often horses) can protect against pathogens or toxins. About 10 percent of the people who receive animal serum are allergic to its proteins.[3]

Children Get Many Shots. What Are They, and Do They Work?

The Centers for Disease Control and Prevention and the American Academy of Pediatrics recommend vaccinations against diphtheria, tetanus and pertussis (whooping cough), polio, measles, mumps, and rubella, influenza, varicella (chicken pox), *Haemophilus influenzae* type b (Hib), and hepatitis B. The vaccines should be given before the age of five or six. Many doctors also recommend vaccinating children against rotavirus. The rotavirus stomach flu is the most common cause of vomiting, diarrhea, and dehydration in young children.

All these vaccines sound like a large number of shots, but the total is not as large as you might think because several are given at once. Examples are the DTP for diphtheria, tetanus, and pertussis and the MMR for measles, mumps, and rubella.

The vaccines are not all the same:

- Polio vaccine comes in two forms. Because the live vaccine can occasionally bring on the disease, most doctors use the inactivated version first.
- DTP: The D and T parts are modified toxins called toxoids. Toxoids induce the immune system to make antibodies that bind the toxin. Long-term, active immunity results. The P in DTP is made from purified parts of the bacteria that causes pertussis (whooping cough).

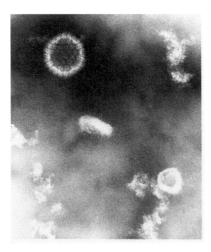

- MMR: All three are live, attenuated viruses.
- Hib: This vaccine is not made from a protein but from a sugar present in the bacterial capsule. This vaccine protects against meningitis and some forms of pneumonia.
- Varicella (chicken pox): Made from live, attenuated virus, this vaccine was licensed in 1995.

Varicella, the virus that causes chicken pox, magnified 275,000 times

- Rotavirus: The Food and Drug Administration approved this live virus vaccine in 1998. It is given by mouth in the early months of life. It may be given at the same time as other vaccines.

Do Teens and Adults Need Shots? Vaccines aren't just for kids. Certain immunizations, such as diphtheria and tetanus, require boosters. Other vaccinations must be repeated annually. A new flu shot comes out every year—not because immunity fades but because flu viruses are constantly mutating.

Because people who go abroad encounter diseases that are not common at home, they may get vaccines against yellow fever, cholera, typhoid, and several others, depending on where they are going. Measles, mumps, and chicken pox can be far more serious diseases in adults than in children. That's why doctors recommend those vaccines for adults who aren't immune. Certain at-risk adults—such as those with asthma or the elderly—need pneumonia vaccines, too.

I Hear So Many Confusing Things About Hepatitis. What's Really Going On? The word hepatitis simply means "inflammation of the liver." Alcohol, drugs, or pollution can cause it. Sometimes it happens for no obvious reason. There's no way to vaccinate against noninfectious hepatitis.

Hepatitis caused by a virus is a different matter. Five types are known to cause hepatitis.[4] They are named with letters A through E. Each has its own mode of transmission. Each has its own set of health problems.

Fever, nausea, vomiting, and diarrhea are often the first symptoms of hepatitis A. Jaundice (a yellowing of the skin and eyes) follows, as the liver fails. The CDC estimates that 143,000 new cases of hepatitis A are reported annually in the United States. The disease strikes 10 million people worldwide each year.[5] Hepatitis A spreads through food or water contaminated by people who are sick with the disease. No healthy carriers are known. Hepatitis A is the most common preventable disease among travelers in the Caribbean, Central and South America, Africa, Asia (but not Japan), Eastern Europe, and the Middle East.

Some 350 million people worldwide are infected with the hepatitis B virus.[6] About 1.2 million Americans carry it. About one in three has no symptoms.[7] Hepatitis B causes jaundice, loss of appetite, and bowel pains. It can lead to liver cancer or cirrhosis (a buildup of fat and scar tissue). Some people cannot completely clear the virus from their bodies. It remains active, making its seemingly healthy carrier capable of infecting others. The disease spreads through blood and body fluids. Like AIDS, sexual contact and shared needles are the prime means of transmission. Worldwide, one person in twenty is a carrier.[8] There is no cure for hepatitis B, but a vaccine can prevent it and drugs are used to treat it.

Hepatitis C spreads mostly through blood or unsterilized needles. Approximately 4 million Americans carry the hepatitis C virus.[9] Most don't know it. There is no vaccine that prevents hepatitis C, but effective treatments are available. The trouble is that most people don't seek treatment because they don't know they have the disease. Symptoms may be few, but hepatitis C can lead to death from liver failure or circulatory problems. The American Association for the Study of Liver Diseases predicts a doubling of liver deaths and a fivefold increase in the need for liver transplants by 2008 unless ways are found to stop hepatitis C.[10]

Hepatitis D affects only those who were previously infected with B. Infection can occur at the same time or later. Like B, the D type spreads through sexual activity and drug use.

Hepatitis E is not spread by carriers. It occurs most often in Africa, Southeast Asia, Pakistan, and countries lying along the Indian Ocean. It spreads in water or food.

Vaccines can prevent types A, B, and D.

Do Vaccines Really Work?

Study this table of data for the United States alone.[11] Then see if you can answer that question for yourself.

Disease	Number of cases in worst year	Number of cases in 1996
Birth defects from rubella	20,000 (1964–65)	2
Diphtheria	206,939 (1921)	1
Measles	894,134 (1941)	494
Mumps	152,209 (1968)	666
Pertussis (whooping cough)	265,269 (1934)	6911
Polio (paralytic)	21,269 (1952)	1
Rubella	57,686 (1969)	210

Why Do Some Vaccines Require Booster Shots and Others Don't?

Experts aren't sure, but the difference may have something to do with memory cells. If too few are made or if too many die, immunity may not last. Another idea is that plasma cells fail to settle in the bone marrow after a low-dose exposure to a pathogen. In some vaccine tests, memory cells show up in bone marrow only after a booster shot. Maybe long-term immunity requires the migration of plasma cells to bone marrow, where memory cells can be formed.

Is It Possible to Vaccinate Against Cancer?

Stephen S. Hall explains why vaccinating against cancer seems like a good idea:

> Cancer cells teeter on the edge between "self" and "not self." As a tumor grows, crowding neighboring cells, it evolves, apparently reactivating genes used in fetal development. Rather than seeing a threatening stranger, as it does when it encounters a flu virus, the immune system sees only a wayward uncle—a bit odd, perhaps, but a relative nonetheless.... The immune system is said to be "tolerant" of the slight differences shown by cancer cells. Immunologists therefore speak of "breaking tolerance"—of overriding this forgiving relationship and nudging the immune system into recognizing cancer as the threat that it is.[12]

The immune system needs this nudge because it cannot always detect cancer cells. Cancer inside a cell can develop without sending any "foreign" antigens to the surface. To the immune system, the cell appears "a bit odd" but permissible.

Like antibiotic-resistant bacteria, tumor cells are constantly changing. Those that can escape the immune defenses survive and multiply. "There is constant competition among the tumor cells," explains Belgian geneticist Thierry Boon, "for the one that is going to be a little more malignant than the others, multiply a bit better, invade [surrounding tissues] a bit better."[13]

An anticancer vaccine, therefore, needs to trick the immune system into destroying cells that look normal. In theory, that trick might be performed in any of several ways. The simplest is to grind up some of the patient's own tumor cells and inject them back into the body. T cells can detect their previously hidden proteins and trigger an immune response. Once the foreign proteins of the cancer are identified, the immune system destroys whole tumor cells. It works in mice. It might also work in people. So might using the patient's tumor cells treated with radiation or drugs that produce mutations.

Another idea is a DNA vaccine against cancer. Researchers in New York worked with mice that had a kind of skin cancer called melanoma. The tumor cells contained a protein called gp75. The immune systems of the mice tolerated the gp75 protein. To break that tolerance, the scientists put the DNA that codes for the human form of gp75 into some cells of the animals' skin. The DNA caused the mouse cells to manufacture human gp75. The human form was just different enough from that of the mouse to launch antibody production. Once antibodies began to attack the human gp75, they also attacked the abnormal mouse gp75 in the tumors.

Protein fragments might work in a similar way. For example, some tumor cells display on their surfaces a protein piece called MAGE-3. It may be possible to inject cancer patients with the MAGE-3 protein and invoke a T cell response that will kill cancer cells. MAGE-3 is not the only candidate for such a vaccine.

Another idea is gene therapy. GM-CSF is a cytokine. It signals helper T cells to rush to the site of an infection. If the gene that controls the production of GM-CSF could be coaxed inside even a few tumor cells, T cells might migrate to the tumor and destroy it.

Why Does It Take So Long to Develop and Approve a Vaccine?

Researchers need many years in the laboratory to develop a vaccine. They need years more to test it—first in animals, then in human volunteers. Government officials and scientists must make sure that vaccines are both safe and effective. Safe means only a few, mild side effects in a very small number of people. (No medical intervention is totally free of risk.) Effective means that the vaccine does what it is supposed to do. It stimulates the right kind of immunity in most of those who get it.

Can Diseases Become Extinct Like the Dinosaurs Did? Smallpox became extinct but not at the hand of nature. Human beings drove the *Variola* (smallpox) virus to extinction in less than two centuries.

In 1895, Sweden announced an ambitious program to vaccinate every citizen against smallpox. Other countries followed Sweden's lead. By the 1930s, Puerto Rico, the Soviet Union, Great Britain, and the Philippines had eliminated smallpox inside their borders. By the 1940s, it seemed the United States had joined the list, but three cases appeared unexpectedly in New York in 1947. A massive vaccination campaign inoculated more than 3 million New Yorkers in a little over a month. No further cases developed in the United States.

Other nations weren't so lucky. Smallpox continued to kill in 31 countries. In the mid-1960s, it was still infecting as many as 15 million people annually. Nearly 2 million died each year. Millions of others survived either disfigured or blinded.[14]

In 1966 the World Health Organization (WHO), an agency of the United Nations, set a goal: the total eradication of smallpox worldwide by 1977. WHO had a powerful, new weapon to use in the fight: a freeze-dried vaccine. This vaccine did not need refrigeration. It could be easily shipped and stored in remote, tropical regions. Still, many problems had to be solved. Many of those nations who needed help most were also the world's poorest. Their transportation systems and health facilities were either inadequate or nonexistent.

Vaccinating everyone was impossible in some countries. What worked better was the idea of "surveillance and containment." The moment that health workers heard of an outbreak, they rushed to the site and vaccinated all who might have been exposed. That strategy worked. Smallpox disappeared quickly in many African countries.

In parts of Asia, smallpox continued to kill. In 1974 it took the lives of more than 25,000 people in India.[15] Indian health workers had to overcome religious objections to vaccination. They gave food and shelter to traveling beggars to prevent them from spreading the contagion. Their efforts paid off. By mid-1975, India was free of smallpox.

In 1978 tragedy struck. A photographer was accidentally infected while taking pictures at a laboratory in Birmingham, England. Hers was the last known death from smallpox.

In 1979 the world breathed a sigh as WHO made its announcement. After 3,000 years, smallpox no longer existed on planet Earth. If no one has the disease, then there's no way to catch it. That meant vaccinations could stop. Today, no child bears the circular scar on the arm that marked those vaccinated against smallpox before 1980.

Only one source of infection remains: the stock cultures maintained in laboratories. Could an accidental infection like the one in Birmingham happen again? Many countries have destroyed their supply of the virus voluntarily. Others have sent their cultures to high-security containment facilities in the United States and Russia. In 1986, 1990, and again in 1994, WHO urged that those last stocks be destroyed to eliminate the final fear: the use of the smallpox virus as a biological weapon, perhaps in the hands of terrorists.

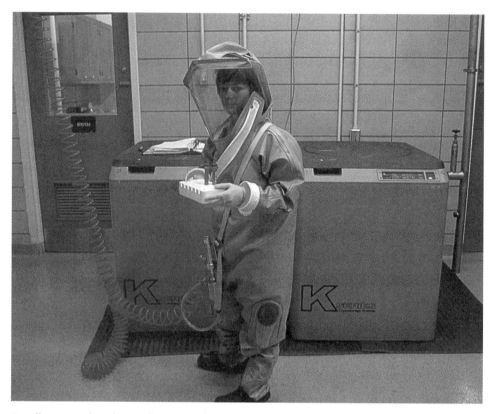

A well-protected worker at the Centers for Disease Control and Prevention

The scientific community stands divided on the recommendation. Some scientists oppose total annihilation. They believe the virus may be valuable for research in the future. "We're taking an extremely precious resource and destroying it," says Bernard Fields of Harvard Medical School.[16] Others think that research can be done on different viruses or on DNA fragments cloned from the smallpox virus. "There are a lot of nuts in the world, and I would just as soon get rid of [the virus]," says MIT immunologist David Baltimore.[17]

Debate continues.

Will You Search for an AIDS Vaccine?

· · · · ·

If science is one part inspiration, . . . and a second part tenaciousness, . . . the third part is the proof, the long, hard benchwork Thomas Edison must have been thinking of when he described genius as 98 percent perspiration.

ROBERT GALLO, A DISCOVERER OF HIV

· · · · ·

*I*magine yourself in a laboratory. You're wearing a white coat. Goggles protect your eyes. All around you, solutions bubble in flasks. Centrifuges spin and whir. You smell ether and ammonia. Computer monitors flicker, stacking numbers into columns and plotting graphs with squiggly lines. You are a scientist, and this is your laboratory. Like thousands of other researchers, you want to stop AIDS. But where will you begin?

An old newspaper lies open on a lab bench. Headlines tell the story of a small child in Los Angeles. Born to an infected mother, the boy tested positive for HIV at 19 days of life and again at 51 days, but by his first birthday, HIV had vanished from his blood. At age five, he was still virus-free and healthy.

When you first read about him, you thought somebody made a mistake. Maybe a laboratory sample became contaminated. Perhaps a careless technician mixed up the results. But soon, similar reports came from other places. The boy in Los Angeles wasn't the only baby to have rid his system of HIV.

A global picture of adults and children living with HIV/AIDS

What might explain such a finding? It's possible that the mother passed anti-HIV antibodies on to her child, perhaps in breast milk. The antibodies might have done for the infant what they could not do for the mother: clear the virus from the blood. Yet another possibility is that the virus may still be there but undetectable in blood tests. Perhaps viruses can "hide" in lymph tissues, remaining invisible for a while but causing AIDS years later.

These ideas fail to satisfy you. You think there's more to the story. Infants aren't the only ones who appear to escape HIV infection. A small number of adults never become infected, even though they are exposed many times. You can think of at least four reasons why this might happen:

- An inherited difference in the immune system prevents HIV from infecting T cells.

- An inherited difference in the immune system destroys T cells after they have been infected, while sparing healthy cells.

- The exposure has been to a low dose or a variant form of the virus that has stimulated a successful immune response.

- The virus strain is defective—unable either to enter blood cells or to multiply once inside.

In 1996 researchers at the National Cancer Institute found the first type. HIV has to lock onto a certain protein on helper T cells in order to infect them. Some people have mutant proteins on their T cells. HIV can't attach, so it can't enter.

Gene Shearer and Mario Clerici at the National Cancer Institute found evidence of the second type. They studied people at high risk for AIDS: gay men, people who inject drugs, babies born to infected mothers, and health-care workers who had been accidentally jabbed by a contaminated needle. Some of these people did not have HIV antibodies in their blood, but about one-third to two-thirds (depending on the risk group) showed evidence of cell-mediated immunity.[18] Their bodies had some ability to destroy infected cells.

Evidence of the third type may have been found, too. The AIDS virus we see most in the United States is HIV-1. Another form is HIV-2, found mostly in West Africa. In a few people, infection with HIV-2 seems to protect against infection with the more deadly HIV-1. One study in Senegal found that women already infected with HIV-2 were three times less likely to get HIV-1 than virus-free women were. Both viruses attach themselves to the same place on the outside of the cell. Maybe HIV-2 doesn't bind as tightly as HIV-1, so it has a harder time working its way in. It's also possible that HIV-2 kick starts the immune system into recognizing proteins shared by both forms.

Evidence of the fourth possibility first came from the land of boomerangs and kangaroos. In the early 1980s a young Australian who didn't know he was infected donated blood. Seven people received his blood and also became infected; but 10 to 14 years later none had developed any AIDS symptoms. Why? In 1995 researchers reported that the Australian virus contains a mutant gene. The gene, named "nef," normally helps the virus infect cells. The mutant nef doesn't work. It cripples the virus.

As you work in your laboratory, you wish you could develop a vaccine to prevent AIDS. Your research efforts will not be the first. In the fight against AIDS, many different vaccines have been tried. Jonas Salk, the inventor of the polio vaccine, made an attempt. He killed HIV with radiation and chemicals and stripped its outer protein coat. He gave the vaccine to HIV-positive people who had not yet developed symptoms. In 1993 he reported his results. The vaccine stimulated antibodies, just as he had hoped it would. It also kept the number of viruses in the blood from rising, and that seemed like good news, too. The rest of the news was bad. The vaccine neither slowed the disease nor lessened the severity of its symptoms.

Later, hopes were dashed when the experimental vaccine gp120 failed to prevent infection in volunteers. The vaccine was a protein made in the lab to mimic one on the surface of HIV. In noninfected volunteers, the vaccine stimulated antibodies that attacked and killed HIV in a test tube, but the same thing failed to happen in real life.

Researchers at Dana-Farber Cancer Institute in Boston report that experiments with live, weakened forms of an HIV-like virus have consistently failed. The scientists deleted some genes involved in viral replication, including the "nef" gene.

They thought the virus would be too weak to cause AIDS. In lab animals the vaccine failed. The virus mutated quickly and grew in the animals. Says project leader Dr. Ruth Ruprecht, "It is not safe to conduct human tests of AIDS vaccines made from live, weakened viruses."[19]

Why has HIV proved so crafty in stumping the vaccine makers? First, the virus exists in many different forms, each with its own proteins. Some 700 variants of HIV have been cataloged. More are added to the list every year. New varieties form when genetic material gets shuffled among different forms infecting the same person.

Second, HIV changes its proteins rapidly. When an HIV-fighting drug enters the bloodstream, a form resistant to the drug can replace the original virus in as little as two weeks.

Third, HIV can "hide" from the immune system. In one study, surgeons removed enlarged adenoids from the throats of 13 patients suspected of having cancer. They found large numbers of HIV in the adenoids. Eleven of the patients didn't even know they were infected.[20]

Another problem is that, when the immune system swings into action to fight another disease, HIV multiplies even faster than usual. Scientists at the National Institute of Allergy and Infectious Diseases gave tetanus booster shots to volunteers. Some were HIV-positive, and some were not. All had been vaccinated against tetanus as children. The immune systems of the non-HIV volunteers produced antibodies against tetanus, as expected. So did the infected people, but millions of HIV particles flooded their bloodstreams as well. That might explain why people in Africa, who are exposed to many more infectious diseases than Americans and Europeans, die five times faster from AIDS—even when they get the same medical treatment.

Will you take the risk and commit years of your life to the search for a vaccine, knowing that the successes of AIDS research have been accompanied by more than a few failures? "Despite a decade of research on AIDS, the medical community has no remedy for it or defense against it," charged *Fortune* in 1994.[21] That same year, the National Institutes of Health (NIH) decided not to fund trials of the leading AIDS vaccines

then under development. Writes Jon Cohen in *Science*: "The move underlined a stark and sober message: A decade had passed since HIV had been unmasked as the cause of AIDS, yet researchers had not even found a vaccine promising enough to justify the expense of a full-scale test. The field lost what little momentum it had."[22]

Four years later, the NIH took steps to revive the dying field of AIDS vaccine research. A new leader took over the NIH's Office of AIDS Research. He announced plans to speed vaccine development with more money, better evaluation of proposals, and increased cooperation with other nations. The NIH also said it would cooperate in vaccine trials being conducted by at least one private company. The vaccine was gp120, one of those that NIH rejected in 1994.

You scratch your head and wonder if a DNA vaccine would work against HIV. If you could get a piece of foreign DNA into infected cells, it might cause the cell to make a protein that the immune system could recognize as "not self." That might induce killer Ts to gobble up the infected cell. Such a vaccine wouldn't prevent AIDS, but it might be a good treatment.

You scratch your head again and wonder if something else might work better. Should you write a proposal? Start an experiment of your own or help in someone else's? Those centrifuges whir. Those solutions bubble. You must make a decision. You must make it soon. Will you search for an AIDS vaccine?

· · · · ·

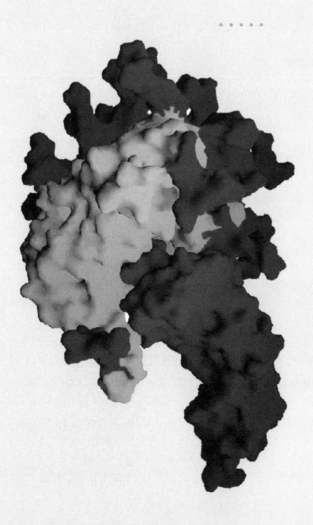

A model of the gp120 molecule: The idea was to ignore the frustrating variety of HIV-1's protein coat, which allowed it to "hide," and create a model of the core section of the virus, which is a constant in all strains of HIV-1.

IN CLOSING

MORE QUESTIONS THAN ANSWERS

The immune system is designed to root out pathogens such as viruses and bacteria with a ferocity that makes it every bit as powerful a force of nature as a hurricane or a volcano.

• STEPHEN S. HALL •

What have you thought about as you have read the questions and answers on these pages? Perhaps you have been struck by how complex your immune system is. It's hard at work when you are sick. It's on the job when you are well, too—invisible, silent, powerful. Human life depends on immunity. You couldn't survive without it. Yet our knowledge of its basis is barely a century old, and we are perhaps centuries more away from a full understanding.

The immune system is so complicated, how can anyone possibly explain it all? The truth is, no one can. Today in laboratories all over the world, scientists are striving to unlock the secrets of the immune system—secrets that could prolong life and promote health for generations to come.

Did you notice that every answer only raised more questions? No matter how far we have come in understanding immunity, we still have a long way to go. The immune system that we take for granted until it goes wrong holds more mysteries than researchers can begin to solve.

Probing the secrets of the cell is like exploring distant galaxies. We have a general idea of the terrain, but our maps are limited until we can get a closer look. With each passing year, our eyes, our instruments, and our experiments probe farther and farther past what we know into a world we can only imagine. The frontiers of space exploration are distant galaxies, pulsars, and supernovas only giant telescopes can bring into view. The frontiers of medical science are molecules and atoms we can't see, even with our most powerful microscopes.

Look back at page 9 and read again what Victor Hugo said about telescopes and microscopes. Which do *you* think has the grander view? How far can you see? How much can you know?

TABLE 1

Immune responses occur in every part of the body. Certain organs and tissues play a major role.

NAME	MISSION
Skin	A nearly impenetrable barrier against pathogens; contains antigen-presenting cells and antibodies.
Sebum, sweat, tears, saliva, mucus	Contain antibodies and enzymes that destroy invaders.
Tonsils and adenoids	Barriers to infection through the nose and mouth.
Stomach	Acid destroys many invaders of the digestive system.
Cilia in airways	Expel dirt, dust, and microbes.
Bone marrow	Contains stem cells that make all blood cells, including white blood cells (leukocytes); also site of maturation for B cells.
Lymph	The fluid that circulates through lymph vessels and carries lymphocytes (B and T cells).
Lymphatic vessels	Carry lymph to all parts of the body.
Lymph nodes	Filter microbes from lymph.
Thymus	Site where lymphocytes mature into T cells.
Peyer's patches	An aggregate of lymph nodes in the intestines that filter microbes from lymph.
Spleen	Filters microbes from lymph.
Spleen and liver	With bone marrow, sites of lymphocyte production.

TABLE 2

The cells of the immune system. Although all are called
white blood cells (leukocytes), nearly all work outside the
bloodstream in the body tissues, as well as in the blood.

NAME	MISSION
Stem cells	Located primarily in the bone marrow; "parents" of all blood cells, including leukocytes.
Phagocytes, including monocytes, macrophages, and dendritic cells	Consume invaders and display their antigens on cell membrane. The display attracts T cells. Phagocytes also clean up dead cells and debris. Dendritic cells are important regulators of immune functions.
Granulocytes, including neutrophils, eosinophils, basophils, and mast cells	Perform many different functions, from releasing enzymes that kill bacteria to combating worm parasites. Most are involved in inflammation and may also cause autoimmune disease.
B cells, plasma cells	B cells become plasma cells. Plasma cells manufacture antibody molecules specific to a single antigen. B cells are primarily responsible for humoral immunity.
Helper T cells (also called CD4 cells)	Inspect foreign proteins presented on cell surfaces; trigger antibody production by B cells; the cells infected by HIV.
Suppressor T cells	Regulate the immune response by decreasing antibody production.
Killer T cells (also called CD8 cells or cytotoxic T cells)	Destroy cancer cells and cells infected with viruses (cell-mediated immunity); also a major factor in transplant rejection.
Natural killer cells	Dissolve the membranes of abnormal cells. Along with killer T cells, NKs are powerful weapons against cancer cells and cells infected with viruses.
Memory cells	Retain the instructions for antibody production against previously encountered antigens; stored in lymph nodes.

TABLE 3

The chemical substances of the immune system.
These chemicals are weapons against invaders, or they carry
messages that regulate immune responses.

NAME	RANK	MISSION
Antibodies (also called immunoglobulins)	Protein	Made by plasma cells (B cells), these Y-shaped proteins bind to an antigen, inactivating it or flagging it for destruction by phagocytes.
Cytokine	Protein	Any one of a class of messenger molecules—secreted by macrophages or lymphocytes—that activates any one of several immune responses.
Interferon (any of several forms including alpha, beta, and gamma)	Cytokine	Involved in fighting viruses and destroying cancer cells. Interferons produced by infected cells protect healthy cells from infection.
Interleukin (any of several forms differentiated by number, such as IL-1, IL-2, etc.)	Cytokine	Interleukin-2 makes T cells multiply. Several interleukins play a part in the inflammatory response.
Complement	A series of enzymes	These enzymes help remove antigen-antibody complexes from the body, activate macrophages, destroy dead cells, and prepare bacterial cells for digestion by macrophages.

NOTES

Chapter One

1. J.H.L. Playfair, *Immunology at a Glance,* 6th ed. (Oxford: Blackwell Science, 1996), p. 16.

2. Gregory Beck and Gail S. Habicht, "Immunity and the Invertebrates," *Scientific American* (November 1996), p. 61.

3. National Institute of Allergy and Infectious Diseases, National Institutes of Health, "The Common Cold," Fact Sheet at http://www.niaid.nih.gov/factsheets/cold.htm.

4. *Ibid.*

5. NIAID says 30 to 35 percent. The 50 percent figure appears in "Common Cold Caused by Multiple Viruses," press release from the American Society for Microbiology, February 3, 1998, at http://www.newswise.com/articles/COLD.ASM.html. Rossmann at Purdue says 70 percent.

6. "Purdue Finding May Snuff Out the Sniffles," press release from Purdue University, April 14, 1998, at http://www.newswise.com/articles/1998/4/SNIFFLES.PUR.html.

7. Mark P. Friedlander and Terry M. Phillips, *The Immune System: Your Body's Disease-Fighting Army* (Minneapolis: Lerner, 1998), p. 95.

8. Carol Kreck, "Running Dry: National Jewish Medical and Research Center Is Desperately Short on Lifesaving Medication for Patients with Immune Deficiency Disorders," *Denver Post* (March 12, 1998), p. E-01.

9. Quoted in Robert S. Desowitz, *The Thorn in the Starfish: The Immune System and How It Works* (New York: W. W. Norton, 1987), p. 39. (Source not cited.)

10. "Plant Viruses Discover How to Overcome Gene Silencing," press release from Washington State University, November 17, 1998, at http://www.newswise.com/articles/VIRUS.WSU.html.

11. Ellen Hale, "Apoptosis Emerging as Hottest Field of Medical Science, Stunning Researchers," Gannett News Service, January 1, 1997, p. S12.

12. Quoted in Ellen Hale, *ibid*.

13. Quoted in Ricki Lewis, "Apoptosis Activity: Cell Death Establishes Itself as a Lively Research Field," *The Scientist* (February 6, 1995), pp. 15–16.

14. Dan Vergano, "Natural-Born Killers," *Science News* (February 8, 1997), p. 88.

15. Aby Mathew, William Hollister, and Robert G. Van Buskirk, "Mysteries of Cell Death: Murder or Suicide?" *The World & I* (April 1, 1997), p. 190.

16. Sharon Begley with Mary Hager and Adam Rogers, "The Cancer Killer," *Newsweek* (December 23, 1996), p. 42.

17. Quoted in "Mystery of Cell Death," University of Iowa press release, October 8, 1998, at http://www.newswise.com/articles/APOTOSIS.UIM.html. (sic APOTOSIS)

Chapter Two

1. Adapted from T.H. Holmes and R.H. Rahe, "The Social Re-adjustment Rating Scale," *Journal of Psychosomatic Research*, vol. 11 (1967), pp. 213–218.

2. Paul Recer, "Stress Factor Seen in Breast Cancer: Study Links Anxiety to Low Immunity," Associated Press, *Denver Post* (January 7, 1998), p. A-19.

3. "Stress Slows Healing of Dental Wounds by 40 Percent," press release from Ohio State University, June 20, 1998.

4. Paul Recer, Associated Press. "Researchers Link Hormones of Stress with Disease," *The Detroit News* (November 16, 1996).

5. Sources disagree in the details of Mary's story.

6. Alan M. Kraut, *Silent Travelers: Germs, Genes, and the "Immigrant Menace"* (Baltimore: Johns Hopkins University Press, 1995), p. 47.

7. Marla Cone, "Defenses Down: Pollution's Toll on Immunity Against Disease—Human Immune Systems May Be Pollution Victims," *Los Angeles Times* (May 13, 1996), pp. A1ff.

8. Ibid.

9. Ibid.

10. Ibid.

11. Donald P. Tashkin, "Effects of Marijuana on the Lung and Its Immune Defenses," *Secretary's Youth Substance Abuse Prevention Initiative: Resource Papers* (March 1997), Center for Substance Abuse and Prevention, pp. 33–51. Other sources give higher numbers.

12. "Crack Cocaine, Marijuana May Damage Lung's Immune System," summary of a study from the *American Journal of Respiratory and Critical Care Medicine* (December 9, 1997), at http://pslgroup.com/dg/4d1fe.htm.

13. Hal Higdon, "A Step Ahead," *Runner's World* (January 1997), pp. 63–65.

14. Quoted in Higdon, *ibid.*

15. Sally Hayhow, "Super Immunity or Super Hype?" *Vegetarian Times* (December 1994), p. 80.

16. Higdon, see above.

17. "Taking Vitamins: Can They Prevent Disease?" *Consumer Reports* (September 1994), pp. 561–564.

18. J.A. Turner, R.A. Deyo, J.D. Loeser, M. Von Korff, and W.E. Fordyce, "The Importance of Placebo Effects in Pain Treatment and Research," *JAMA, National Library of Medicine Record, MDX Health Digest* (May 25, 1994), page numbers unavailable.

19. Roger Dobson, "Music Tunes the Body into Good Health," *The Sunday Times* (London) (July 27, 1997), Innovation Section.

20. Quoted in Rebecca A. Clay, "Researchers Harness the Power of Humor," *The APA Monitor* (September 1997), at http://www.apa.org/monitor/sep97/humor.html.

21. Susan M. Persons, "Social Support, Stress, and the Common Cold: A Summary of a Presentation by Sheldon Cohen, Ph.D., Carnegie Mellon University," *NIH Record* (December 2, 1997), at http://www1.od.nih.gov/obssr/socsup.html.

22. "First-Ever Scientific Estimate of Total Bacteria on Earth," University of Georgia press release, August 25, 1998, at http://www.newswise.com/articles/BACTERIA2.UGA.html.

23. Gwenda Blair, "Germs Warfare," *Self* (February 1997), pp. 149–150.

24. Garry Hamilton, "Let Them Eat Dirt," *New Scientist* (July 18, 1998), at http://www.newscientist.com/ns/980718/features.html.

25. David Spark, "Science: A Drug for Every Bug," *Independent* (London) (August 5, 1997), pp. N8–N9.

26. Ibid.

27. Clair Wood, "Dirt, Early Exposure to Infection May Prevent Allergies," *Bangor Daily News* (August 10, 1998), page numbers unavailable.

28. Rook, quoted in both Wood and Hamilton.

29. Matt Ridley, "Acid Test: Keep Taking the Soil Tablets," *The Daily Telegraph* (London) (July 20, 1998), PSA-2141.

Chapter Three

1. National Center for Infectious Diseases, Centers for Disease Control and Prevention.

2. Pharmaceutical Research and Manufacturers of America, "Experimental Drugs Against Infectious Diseases," press release, September 16, 1998 at http://www.newswise.com/articles/INFECT.PRM.html.

3. Lennart Nilsson, *The Body Victorious*, (New York: Delacorte, 1985), p. 88.

4. The numbers in this section are calculated from "Comparative Sizes," in J.H.L. Playfair, *Immunology at a Glance*, 6th edition (London: Blackwell, 1996), p. 90.

5. Dianne Hales, "An End to Ulcers," *Woman's Day* (May 17, 1994), p. 66.

6. R. Scott Fritz, "New Insights into the Symptoms and Treatment of Influenza," 38th Interscience Conference on Antimicrobial Agents and Chemotherapy, September 24–27, 1998, San Diego, CA.

7. "Antibiotic Resistant Bacteria: Superbugs Thrive in Hospitals," *Mayo Clinic Health Oasis* (December 7, 1998), at http://www.mayohealth.org/mayo/9812/htm/superbugs.htm.

8. Richard Smith. "Action on Antimicrobial Resistance," *British Medical Journal* (September 19, 1998), p. 764.

9. Paul Raeburn, "Flesh-Destroying Bacteria May Be Return of Deadly 19th Century Germ," *News* (Boca Raton, Florida) (June 9, 1994), p. 2A. Associated Press Newsfeature.

10. Tom Philp, "Flesh-Eating Bacteria Became Parents' Worst Nightmare," *Sacramento Bee* (February 7, 1995), pp. A1ff.

11. Robert G. Whalen, "DNA Vaccines for Emerging Infectious Diseases: What If?" *Emerging Infectious Diseases*, National Center for Infectious Diseases, July-September, 1996, pp. 168–175.

12. "Update: Trends in AIDS Incidence—United States, 1996," *Morbidity and Mortality Weekly Report*, Centers for Disease Control and Prevention (September 19, 1997), page numbers unavailable.

13. Hugh Matthews, "UN Report Warns That AIDS Epidemic Is Still Out of Control," *British Medical Journal* (November 28, 1998), p. 1472.

14. Michael Balter, "How Does HIV Overcome the Body's T Cell Bodyguards?" *Science*, vol. 278 (1399), (November 21, 1997), pp. 1399–1400.

15. "Gene Therapy Tested for HIV," The Associated Press News Service (April 1, 1996), NewsBank, Inc. Record Number 00802*19960401*02890.

16. Armin Brott, "Bone Marrow Report: The Real Medical Miracle," *Family Circle* (October 6, 1998), p.134.

17. "Cord Blood Cells in Adult Bone Marrow Transplants," press release from Loyola University Medical Center, December 8, 1998, at http://www.newswire.com/articles/BONEMARO.LMC.html.

18. Charles Petit, "Oakland AIDS Activist's Latest Crusade: Jeff Getty Fighting for Interspecies Graft," *San Francisco Chronicle* (February 16, 1998), News Section.

19. Gyongyi Szabo, "Alcohol and Susceptibility to Tuberculosis," *Alcohol Health & Research World*, vol. 21, no. 1 (Winter 1997), p. 39.

20. Quoted in Laurie Garrett, *The Coming Plague: Newly Emerging Diseases in a World Out of Balance*, (New York: Farrar, Straus and Giroux, 1994), p. 531.

21. Denise Grady, "Death at the Corners," *Discover* (December 1993), p. 82.

22. Ibid.

23. Garrett, *op. cit.*

1. Berton Roueché, *The Medical Detectives* (New York: Truman Talley Books/ Plume, 1998), p. 306.

2. American Academy of Allergy, Asthma, and Immunology, "Advice from Your Allergist: Rhinitis," updated March 25, 1998, at http://allergy.mcg.edu/advice/rhin.html.

3. If asthma is included, the figure rises to 40 to 50 million, according to the American Academy of Allergy, Asthma, and Immunology.

4. Cynthia Cooney, "Doctor Aids Allergy Sufferers," *Westchester (Illinois) Herald* (July 15, 1998).

5. R.F. Horan, L.S. Schneider, and A.L. Sheffer. "Allergic Skin Disorders and Mastocytosis," *Journal of the American Medical Association* (November 25, 1992), pp. 3858–3868.

6. Donald Y.M. Leung, Luis A. Diaz, Vincent DeLeo, and Nicholas A. Soter, "Allergic and Immunologic Skin Disorders," *Journal of the American Medical Association* (December 10, 1997), pp. 1914–1924.

7. Ibid.

8. American College of Allergy, Asthma, and Immunology, "Insect Sting Allergies Pose Serious Risk," *Bulletin* (May 29, 1998), p. 1, at http://allergy.mcg.edu/news/insects.html.

9. M.D. Valentine. "Anaphylaxis and Stinging Insect Hypersensitivity," *Journal of the American Medical Association* (November 25, 1992), pp. 2830–2833.

10. American College of Allergy, Asthma, and Immunology, *op. cit.*

11. J.J. Van Gasse, *What Am I Allergic To?* (Ann Arbor: Proctor Publications, 1995), p. 23.

12. Richard D. DeShazo and Stephen F. Kemp, "Allergic Reactions to Drugs and Biologic Agents," *Journal of the American Medical Association* (December 10, 1997), pp. 1895–1906.

13. Quoted in "Vaccination Can Prevent Allergy Symptoms," press release from Public Communications, Inc. (December 8, 1998), at http:www.newswise.com/articles/VACCINAT.PCI.html.

14. Richard W. Weber, "Immunotherapy with Allergens," *Journal of the American Medical Association* (December 10, 1997), pp. 188–194.

15. Hugh A. Sampson, "Food Allergy," *Journal of the American Medical Association* (December 10, 1997), pp. 1888–1894.

16. "Food Allergies and Intolerances," National Institute of Allergies and Infectious Diseases, at http://www.niaid.nih.gov/publications/food/full.html.

17. Hugh A. Sampson, *op. cit.* Sources vary.

18. American College of Allergy, Asthma, and Immunology, "Here's Some Food for Thought," updated November 20, 1996, at http://allergy.mcg.edu/advice/foods.html.

Chapter Five

1. "Definition," Lupus Foundation of America, at http://www.internet-plaza.net/lupus/info/def.html.

2. "Rheumatoid Arthritis: Treatment Options," *Health Oasis: Mayo Clinic.* September 1998, at http://www.mayohealth/org/mayo/9809/htm/rheu.html. Numbers vary slightly among sources.

3. "Identify Possible Connection in JRA," press release from the American College of Rheumatology, October 28, 1998, at http://www.newswise.com/pp/articles/9595.RHM.html.

4. C. M. Verhoef *et al.* "Mutual Antagonism of Rheumatoid Arthritis and Hay Fever: A Role for Type 1/Type 2 Cell Imbalance," *Annals of the Rheumatic Diseases*, 1998, pp. 275–280.

5. "A Fast Track for Diabetes Cure Focused on Islet Cell Transplantation," Harvard Medical School press release, September 15, 1998, at http://www.newswise.com/articles/JDFCENT.HMS.html.

6. Arthur K. Balin, Loretta Pratt Balin, and Marietta Whittlesey, *The Life of the Skin* (New York: Bantam Books, 1997), p. 116.

7. James G. Krueger, "Pathogenesis and Treatment of Psoriasis," Laboratory for Investigative Dermatology: James G. Krueger," at http://www.rockefeller.edu/labheads/krueger/krueger.html.

8. The National Psoriasis Foundation.

9. "Improved Treatment for Autoimmune Diseases," June, 1997, at http://www.allabouthealth.com/Catalog/News/NewsItems/News096.htm.

10. "Multiple Sclerosis: New Leads into Its Cause and Treatment," *Mayo Clinic Health Letter*, January 1998, p. 1, at http://www.mayohealth/org/mayo/9511/htm/multiple.htm. A lower estimate of 300,000 appears in a press release from the University of Pennsylvania Medical Center, "Relapses Prevented in Mouse Multiple Sclerosis Model," October 30, 1998, at http://www.newswise.com/articles/MSMOUSE.UPM.html. Other sources give other numbers.

11. The Scleroderma Foundation and the Scleroderma Research Foundation.

12. Associated Press, "Experimental Treatment Restores Woman's Youth," September 21, 1998, at http://flash.oregonlive.com.

13. NIH, "Mechanisms of Immune Response to Xenotransplant Antigens," *NIH Guide* (August 8, 1997), PA-97-089.

14. Franklin Hoke, "As Cross-Species Transplantations Move Ahead, Some Scientists Call for Caution, Restraint," *The Scientist* (August 21, 1995), p. 1.

15. The FDA says he transplanted a liver. Others say the goat provided a kidney.

16. "Majority of Americans Support Xenotransplantation, NKF Poll Finds," *Transplant News* (February 28, 1998), p. 5

17. Mary Wooley, "Support for Xenotransplants," *The Scientist* (June 23, 1997), pages not available.

18. Quoted in Steven Benowitz, "Scientists View Bone Marrow Xenotransplant with Optimism, Caution," *The Scientist* (March 4, 1996), pp. 3–4.

19. Quoted in Paulette V. Walker, "Regulating Research in Xenotransplantation Proves Difficult for Government," *The Chronicle of Higher Education* (January 31, 1997), p. A24.

Chapter Six

1. Samuel L. Katz, "Future Vaccines and a Global Perspective," *The Lancet* (December 13, 1997), p. 1767.

2. Kathryn Brown, "Vaccine Cuisine," *Environmental Health Perspectives* (March 1996), p. 276.

3. Michael McDonnell and Frederick K. Askari, "Immunization," *Journal of the American Medical Association* (December 10, 1997), pp. 2000–2007.

Baseline data credited to G. Peter, "Childhood Immunizations," *New England Journal of Medicine* (December 17, 1992), pp. 1794–1800.

4. A sixth type, G, is thought not to be clinically significant.

5. Brett Grodeck, "Viral Hepatitis," *Positively Aware* (September/October 1995), pp. 12–15. Estimates from other sources vary.

6. Deborah Josefson, "Oral Treatment for Hepatitis B Gets Approval in United States," *British Medical Journal* (October 17, 1998), p. 1034.

7. Grodeck, *op. cit.*

8. "Project to Develop Edible Plant Vaccine," press release from Roswell Park Cancer Institute, at http://www.newswise.com/articles/VACCINE2.RPC.html.

9. American College of Gastroenterology, "Experts Discuss Viral Hepatitis," press release, October 6, 1998, at http://www.newswise.com/articles/HEP.ACG.html.

10. "U.S. Health Care Burden to Soar Unless Hepatitis Treated," press release from the American Association for the Study of Liver Diseases, November 4, 1998, at http://www.newswise.com/pp/articles/9856.SLD.html.

11. Adapted from McDonnell and Askari, *ibid.* Baseline data credited to G. Peter, "Childhood Immunizations," *New England Journal of Medicine* (1992), pp. 1794–1800.

12. Stephen Hall, "Vaccinating Against Cancer," *Atlantic Monthly* (April 1997), pp. 66ff.

13. Quoted in Hall, *ibid.*

14. "Scene Is Set for Destruction of Smallpox Virus," WHO press release, September 9, 1994.

15. James Cross Giblin, *When Plague Strikes: The Black Death, Smallpox, AIDS* (New York: HarperCollins, 1995), p. 107.

16. Karen Young Kreeger, "Smallpox Extermination Proposal Stirs Scientists," *The Scientist* (November 14, 1994), p. 1.

17. Ibid.

18. G.M. Shearer and M. Clerici, "Protective Immunity Against HIV Infection: Has Nature Done the Experiment for Us?" *Immunology Today* (January 1996), pp. 21–24.

19. "Danger of Vaccines Made from Live, Weakened AIDS Virus Reaffirmed," press release from Dana-Farber Cancer Institute (January 28, 1999), at http://www.newswise.com/pp/articles/10867.DFC.html.

20. S. S. Frankel, B. M. Wenig, A. P. Burke *et al*. "Replication of HIV-1 in Bendritic Cell-Derived Synctia at the Mucosal Surface of the Adenoid," *Science* (May 18, 1996), pp. 115–117.

21. Peter Nulty, "Where All That AIDS Money Is Going," *Fortune* (February 7, 1994), p. 139.

22. Jon Cohen, "NIH Concocts a Booster Shot for HIV Vaccines," *Science* (August 28, 1998), pp. 1270–1271.

GLOSSARY

Acquired immunity: immunity obtained through life experiences, either by vaccination or by having the disease.

Active immunity: long-term immunity conferred through memory cells capable of making antibodies against a particular pathogen.

Adrenal gland: a gland that produces adrenaline and other hormones.

Adrenaline: a stress hormone released by the adrenal gland. Also called *Epinephrine.*

AIDS (Acquired Immune Deficiency Syndrome): a disease characterized by a host of opportunistic infections and cancers arising from a failure of the immune system. The failure results from the infection of helper T cells by HIV (Human Immunodeficiency Virus).

Allergen: any substance that produces an allergic response.

Allergic rhinitis: excess mucus production in airways in response to an allergen.

Allergy: an overreaction of the immune system to a harmless antigen.

Amino acids: the chemical building blocks of proteins.

Anaphylactic shock: an extreme allergic reaction accompanied by a rapid drop in blood pressure and the potential for circulatory failure.

Antibody: a protein that binds to a specific antigen, thereby protecting the body against foreign invaders and (sometimes) causing an allergic reaction.

Antibody: any of several classes of antimicrobial substances.

Antigen: any particle or substance that triggers an immune response.

Antigen-presenting cells: leukocytes that dock antigens to their cell membranes (for inspection by helper T cells).

Antitoxin: a substance that counterattacks a toxin or poison.

Antiviral drug: a drug that combats a virus.

Apoptosis: programmed cell death triggered by proteins and affected by enzymes.

Arthritis: any swelling, pain, or stiffness of joints. See also *Osteoarthritis* and *Rheumatoid arthritis*.

Asthma: a constriction of the bronchial tubes (to the lungs), which causes wheezing sounds and difficulty in breathing.

Atopy: the tendency toward multiple allergies (adjective is *atopic*).

Autoimmune disease: an attack of the immune system on the body's normal cells, tissues, or organs.

AZT (azidothymidine or zidovudine): a drug used to treat AIDS patients.

Bacteria: single-celled organisms lacking a nucleus, a very few of which are pathogens.

Bacteriophage: a virus that infects a bacterial species.

Basophil: a circulating cell that contains histamines, which are released during an allergic reaction. See also *Mast cell* and *Granulocyte*.

B cell: a type of lymphocyte that, after becoming a plasma cell, makes antibodies.

Caspase: any one in a series of enzymes that affects apoptosis.

CD4 cells: see *Helper T cells*.

CD8 cells: see *Killer T cells*.

Cell-mediated immunity: the action of killer T cells and natural killer cells in destroying abnormal cells or cells infected with a virus.

Chemokine: a category of cytokine.

Chemotherapy: the use of powerful drugs to treat cancer.

Complement: enzymes that dissolve invaders and attract other immune cells to the battle.

Cytokines: chemical messengers of the immune system. See Table 3.

Cytotoxic T cell: see *Killer T cell*.

Dendritic cell: an antigen-presenting cell that helps regulate the immune response.

Desensitization: reduction in the allergic response attained by administering small, increasing dosages of allergen over a period of time.

Diabetes: a disease characterized by the failure of the pancreas to produce sufficient insulin, the substance that regulates the body's release of energy from sugar. Type I (juvenile diabetes) is thought to be an autoimmune disorder, in that the immune system attacks and destroys insulin-producing cells.

DNA: see *Genetic material*.

Endogenous virus: a virus that is part of an organism's genetic makeup.

Enzyme: a protein that speeds up a specific chemical reaction within living cells.

Eosinophil: a granulocyte involved in the allergic response.

Epinephrine: See *Adrenaline*.

Fungi: parasites similar to plants but lacking chlorophyll (and therefore incapable of food production).

Gamma globulin: the part of the blood that contains antibodies.

Gene: the fundamental unit of inheritance. A piece of genetic material (usually DNA, sometimes RNA) that carries instructions for the production of a particular protein.

Genetic material: the molecules that carry the instructions for performing the life processes of cells. The molecules are either DNA—or in the case of some viruses, RNA.

Granulocyte: a leukocyte that releases the contents of its vacuoles when a vacuole fuses with the cell membrane. See also *Basophil* and *Mast cell*.

Helper T cell: a kind of lymphocyte that detects foreign proteins and initiates antibody production.

Hepatitis: inflammation of the liver. Forms A through E are viral.

Herd immunity: the immunity conferred upon an individual by virtue of membership in an immune group.

Histamine: a chemical released during an allergic reaction, which causes symptoms such as a rash on the skin or excess mucus in the respiratory system.

Histocompatability antigen: proteins on a cell surface that identify it to the immune system (as either "self" or "not self").

Histocompatability testing: see *Tissue typing*.

HIV (Human Immunodeficiency Virus): the virus that causes AIDS.

HIV test: a laboratory test that detects antibodies against HIV in the blood. At-home tests are also available.

Homeostasis: balance and equilibrium in living systems.

Hormone: a chemical produced by one gland or organ that affects another.

HPA axis: hypothalamus, pituitary, adrenal gland interaction, producing hormones that regulate bodily processes, including immune system functions.

Humoral immunity: the action against pathogens affected by antibodies in blood and lymph.

Hypothalamus: a nerve center in the brain that sends chemical messages to the pituitary, controlling numerous basic functions including immune response.

Immune: protected from disease.

Immune system: all the cells, tissues, and organs involved in the immune response.

Immunity: the ability to escape a disease when exposed to its causative agent.

Immunization: any one of several medical procedures intended to initiate immune system action against a specific disease. Substances used for immunization include vaccines, toxoids, antibodies, or antitoxins.

Immunodeficiency: loss of immune structures and functions.

Immunoglobulin: see *Antibody*.

Immunoglobulin E (IgE): an antibody that binds to mast cells and basophils, causing the release of histamine, which, in turn, brings on allergic symptoms.

Immunoglobulin G (IgG): the most abundant antibody form in human gamma globulin; IgG antibodies prevent or diminish allergic responses.

Immunosuppressive drugs: substances used to block the action of the immune system, usually for the purpose of preventing rejection (immune attack) of a transplanted organ.

Immunotherapy: vaccination against allergy through desensitization.

Inflammation: swelling, redness, and pain associated with a buildup of immune cells and substances around an injury.

Innate immunity: inborn protection against a disease.

Interferon: any of several proteins produced by the immune system in response to a viral attack. Some forms impede the growth of cancer cells.

Interleukin: any of several cytokines that affect immune function.

Killer T cells: T cells that kill cancerous cells or cells infected with a virus.

Leukocyte: any white blood cell.

Ligament: the connective tissue that holds bones together.

Long-term nonprogressors: HIV-positive people who do not develop AIDS symptoms after 10 or more years.

Lupus: see *SLE*.

Lymph: the clear fluid that bathes all body cells and carries immune cells.

Lymph nodes: nodules in the neck, groin, abdomen, and armpits that develop and store white blood cells and filter disease-causing organisms out of the lymphatic circulation.

Lymph vessels: the channels through which lymph circulates.

Lymphocyte: any leukocyte that circulates in lymph—for example, a T cell or a B cell.

Macrophage: a large leukocyte that consumes invading organisms and presents foreign antigens on its membrane.

Mast cell: a stationary cell that releases histamine when bound to IgE during an allergic attack. See also *Basophil* and *Granulocyte*.

Monocyte: a large, circulating phagocyte.

MHC (Major Histocompatibility Complex): any of several types of antigen-binding sites on the membrane of a cell.

Memory cell: a modified plasma or T cell that confers immunity by storing information necessary to antibody production.

Microbe or *microorganism*: a living thing too small to be seen without the aid of a microscope.

Multiple sclerosis (MS): an autoimmune attack on the myelin sheath that covers nerve cells, producing impairment of the muscles and sensory nerves.

Mutation: a change in the genetic material of an organism.

Organism: any living thing.

Osteoarthritis: swelling, stiffness, and pain in the joints brought on by the wear and tear of aging.

Passive immunization: transferring antibodies from one organism to another to achieve short-term immunity.

Parasite: any organism that lives in or on another living thing and extracts its energy and nutritional needs from its host.

Pathogen: any microorganism that causes disease.

Pemphigus: a category of autoimmune diseases of the skin.

Peyer's patches: a group of lymph nodes lying at the juncture of the large and small intestines.

Phagocyte: any of several classes of lymphocyte that consume invading antigens or organisms.

Pituitary gland: a hormone-producing gland in the brain that receives signals from the hypothalamus and helps regulate many physical processes, including sleep, emotions, and immune responses.

Placebo effect: the tendency of a nontherapeutic substance to produce a perceived therapeutic effect among some percentage of its users.

Plasma: the liquid portion of blood.

Plasma cell: a B cell in a form capable of producing antibodies.

Plasmid: a ring of genetic material in a bacterial cell.

Pollen: the male reproductive cells of flowering plants, known to provoke allergic symptoms in sensitive individuals.

Protease inhibitors: drugs that block the action of protease, an enzyme important in the replication of a virus.

Protein: any molecule made of amino acids. Proteins form much of an organism's structure and are responsible for much of its functioning.

Protozoa: microscopic organisms that share some characteristics with animals. Some are pathogens.

Psoriasis: an autoimmune disease of the skin.

Retrovirus: a virus that makes reverse transcriptase and can translate RNA into DNA.

Rhinitis: runny nose.

Receptors: sites on a cell membrane that accept molecules.

Rheumatoid arthritis: an autoimmune disease involving the attack and destruction of tissues of the joints and bones.

RNA: see *Genetic material*.

SCID (Severe Combined Immunodeficiency Disease): a rare, inborn disease of the immune system in which the body is incapable of producing either T or B-lymphocytes.

Scleroderma: an autoimmune disease of the connective tissue.

Serum: clear, fluid portion of blood that remains after clotting. It contains antibodies, which confer passive immunity if injected into another individual.

SLE (Systemic Lupus Erythromatosus): autoimmune disease in which the immune system attacks and destroys cells of the skin, blood vessels, kidneys, and heart.

Stem cells: cells in the bone marrow that manufacture blood cells, including leukocytes.

Suppressor T cells: lymphocytes that slow the immune response after bacterial or viral invaders have been conquered.

T cells: a category of lymphocyte. See: *Killer, Helper,* and *Suppressor* types.

Thymus: a gland behind the breastbone where T cells develop.

Tissue typing: a laboratory test to categorize cell surface proteins for the purpose of antigen matching, as for organ transplants.

Toxoid: a modified toxin used to elicit antibody production against a poison.

Transformation: the transfer of genetic material and characteristics from one strain or species of bacteria to another.

Ulcer: a sore in the stomach or intestine that will not heal. Most are caused by bacteria.

Vacuole: a fluid-filled cavity in a cell.

Vaccination: the administration of any vaccine or toxoid.

Vaccine: a human-made substance that stimulates antibody production and provides future immunity against a disease.

Virus: a particle of genetic material (either DNA or RNA) surrounded by a protein coat.

Xenograft: a transplant of cells or tissues from one species to another.

Xenotransplant: a transplant of a whole organ from one species to another.

FOR FURTHER INFORMATION

ARTICLES

Bartlett, John G., and Richard D. Moore, "Improving HIV Therapy," *Scientific American* (July 1998), pp. 84–87.

Beck, Gregory, and Gail S. Habicht, "Immunity and the Invertebrates," *Scientific American* (November 1996), pp. 60–66.

Begley, Sharon, with Mary Hager and Adam Rogers, "The Cancer Killer," *Newsweek* (December 23, 1996), pp. 42–47.

Blair, Gwenda, "Germs Warfare," *Self* (February 1997), pp. 148–151+.

Brink, Susan, "Beating the Odds (AIDS)," *U.S. News & World Report* (February 12, 1996), pp. 60–68.

Bylinksy, Gene, and Alicia Hills Moore, "Health: Cell Suicide: The Birth of a Mega-Market," *Fortune* (May 15, 1995), pp. 75ff.

Gorman, Christine, "Are Some People Immune to AIDS?" *Time* (March 22, 1993), pp. 49–51.

Gorman, Christine, "A New Attack on AIDS," *Time* (July 8, 1996), pp. 52–53.

Grady, Denise, "Death at the Corners," *Discover* (December 1993), pp. 82ff.

Hall, Stephen S. "Vaccinating Against Cancer," *Atlantic Monthly* (April 1997), pp. 66ff.

Hayhow, Sally, "Super Immunity or Super Hype?" *Vegetarian Times* (December 1994), pp. 80–85.

Higdon, Hal, "A Step Ahead," *Runner's World* (January 1997), pp. 63–65.

Litman, Gary W., "Sharks and the Origins of Vertebrate Immunity," *Scientific American* (November 1996), pp. 67–71.

Newman, Jack, "How Breast Milk Protects Newborns," *Scientific American* (December 1995), pp. 76–79.

Novitt-Morena, Anne. "Antibiotics: What's Happening to Our Miracle Drugs?" *Current Health 2* (December 1995), pp. 6ff.

Nowak, Martin A., and Andrew J. McMichael, "How HIV Defeats the Immune System," *Scientific American* (August 1995), pp. 48ff.

Radetsky, Peter, "Immune to a Plague," *Discover* (June 1997), pp. 60–67.

Radetsky, Peter, "Last Days of the Wonder Drugs," *Discover* (November 1998), pp. 76–85.

Sternberg, Esther M., and Philip W. Gold, "The Mind-Body Interaction in Disease," *Mysteries of the Mind, Scientific American* (Special Issue 7, 1997), pp. 8–15.

Williams, Rebecca D., "Organ Transplants from Animals: Examining the Possibilities," *FDA Consumer* (June 1996), pp. 12–16.

BOOKS AND VIDEOS

Aaseng, Nathan, *Autoimmune Diseases*. New York: Franklin Watts, 1995.

Brynie, Faith Hickman, *AIDS: Facts, Issues, Choices*. Kettering, Ohio: PPI Publishing, 1997.

Clark, William R., *At War Within: The Double-Edged Sword of Immunity*. New York: Oxford University Press, 1995.

Desowitz, Robert S., *The Thorn in the Starfish: The Immune System and How It Works*. New York: W.W. Norton, 1987.

Friedlander, Mark P., and Terry M. Phillips, *The Immune System: Your Body's Disease-Fighting Army*. Minneapolis: Lerner, 1998.

Isenberg, David, and John Morrow, *Friendly Fire: Explaining Autoimmune Disease*. New York: Oxford University Press, 1995.

National Institute of Health, *Understanding Vaccines*. U.S. Department of Health and Human Services, NIH Publication No. 98-4219: January 1998.

Packer, Kenneth L., *HIV Infection: The Facts You Need to Know*. New York: Franklin Watts, 1998.

Radetsky, Peter, *The Invisible Invaders: The Story of the Emerging Age of Viruses*. Boston: Little, Brown, 1991.

Regis, Ed, *Virus Ground Zero: Stalking the Killer Viruses with the Centers for Disease Control*. New York: Pocket Books, 1996.

Science of HIV, The (30-minute video). Washington, DC: National Science Teachers Association, 1997.

Shurkin, Joel N., *The Invisible Fire: The Story of Mankind's Victory Over the Ancient Scourge of Smallpox*. New York: G.P. Putnam, 1979.

ORGANIZATIONS

American Academy of Allergy, Asthma and Immunology
611 East Wells Street
Milwaukee, WI 53202
http://www.aaaai.org/
Distributes pamphlets and brochures.

American College of Allergy, Asthma & Immunology
85 West Algonquin Road, Suite 550
Arlington Heights, IL 60005
http://www.allergy.mcg.edu/
News for patients, physicians, and the media.

American Association of Immunologists
9650 Rockville Pike
Bethesda, MD 20814-3994
http://www.sciencexchange.com/aai/
Publishes *The Journal of Immunology*.

Arthritis Foundation, Inc.
1330 West Peachtree Street
Atlanta, GA 30309
http://www.arthritis.org
Publishes *Arthritis Today* and "Kids Get Arthritis Too."

Asthma and Allergy Foundation of America
1125 15th Street NW, Suite 502
Washington, DC 20005
http://www.aafa.org
Distributes educational materials. Maintains local chapters.

Asthma Information Center
American Medical Association
515 North State Street
Chicago, IL 60610
http://www.ama-assn.org/special/asthma/
Provides educational materials. Sponsors support groups.

CDC National Prevention
Information Network
P.O. Box 6003
Rockville, MD 20849-6003
http://www.cdcnac.org
The nation's most complete
collection of references on AIDS,
sexually transmitted diseases, and
tuberculosis.

Hepatitis Foundation International
30 Sunrise Terrace
Cedar Grove, NJ 07009-1423
http://www.hepfi.org
The video *Respect Yourself – Protect
Yourself* tells how to avoid hepatitis
B and C.

Immune Deficiency Foundation
25 West Chesapeake Avenue,
Suite 206
Towson, MD 21204
http://www.primaryimmune.org/
Publishes a handbook for families.

Lupus Foundation of America
1300 Piccard Drive, Suite 200
Rockville, MD 20850-4303
http://www.internet-plaza.net/lupus/
info/about/index/html
Maintains local chapters nation-
wide. Publishes "Lupus News."

National Foundation for Infectious
Diseases
4733 Bethesda Avenue, Suite 750
Bethesda, MD 20814
http://www.nfid.org
Publishes a newsletter, "The Double
Helix."

National Institute of Allergy and
Infectious Diseases (NIAID)
Office of Communications
Building 31, Room 7A-50
31 Center Drive, MSC2520
Bethesda, MD 20892-2520
http://www.niaid.nih.gov/
Provides free pamphlets and news
releases on allergies.

National Multiple Sclerosis Society
733 Third Avenue
New York, NY 10017
http://www.nmss.org/
Call 1-800-FIGHT MS for
information.

National Psoriasis Foundation
6600 SW 92nd Avenue, Suite 300
Portland, OR 97223
http://www.psoriasis.org/
Distributes free informational
packets on psoriasis.

The Living Bank
Organ Donor Registry
Box 6725
Houston, TX 77265
http://www.livingbank.org
Publishes a newsletter, "The Bank
Account."

United Network for Organ Sharing
National Transplantation Resource
Center
1100 Boulders Parkway, Suite 500
Richmond, VA 23225
http://www.unos.org/
Keeps up-to-date statistics on organ
transplants.

INDEX

cell-mediated immunity, 32, 33, 55, 117, 143
cellular suicide, 42–43, *44*, 45
Chagas' disease, 109
chemical reactions, 10, 19
chemokines, 31, 32
chemotherapy, 85
childbirth, 116
cilia, *16*, 17, 149
colds, 28, 55, 57, 58, 95
collagen, 115
colony-stimulating factors, 31, 32
complement system, 11, 15, 19, 30, 50, 70, 151
conjugate vaccines, 127
cortisol, 47, 57
CRH, 47
cytokines, 15, 31, 32, 38, 46, 47, 48, 55, 63, 70, 71, 96, 115, 151
cytotoxic T cells (*see* killer T cells)

dendritic cells, 20, *21*, 150
desensitization, 102
diabetes mellitus, 107, 112–113
diet, 58–60
DNA, 26, 27, 30, 36, 43, 67, 76, 109, 128, 137, 145, 146
dopamine, 120
drug allergies, 101, 102
drugs, 55, 60

Ebola virus, 77–78
edible vaccines, 129, *130*
enzymes, 10, 11, 19, 20, 43
eosinophils, *21*, 22, 96, 150

erythromycin, 73
estrogen, 116, 117
exercise, 57–58, 60

Fas, 43
fetus, 50, 119
fever, 71, 72
fight or flight response, 48–49, 56
filovirus, 77
flatworms, 67, 68
flesh-eating bacteria, 77
flu virus, *75*
folic acid, 58, 59
food allergies, 104–106
food intolerance, 104, 105
fungi, 26, 67, 68, 93, *94*

gamma globulin, 37
gene silencing, 40
gene therapy, *36*, 36–37, 83–84
genetic differences, 26
genetic engineering, 122
genetic material (*see* DNA; RNA)
glucose, *58*
GM-CSF, 137
Goodpasture syndrome, 108
gp75, 137
gp120, 144, 145, *146*
granulocytes, 20, 22, 150
Graves' disease, 107
growth factors, 31, 32, 70

hantavirus, 78, 89–91
Hashimoto disease, 107
hay fever, 63, 95, 96, 98
Helicobacter pylori, 70
helper T cells, 19, 27, 30, 33, 63, 81, 82, 84, 109, 117, 126, 143, 150

hepatitis, 53, 133–135
herd immunity, 26
herpes, 53, 122
histamine, 22, 31, 63, 92, 98, 99, 102
histocompatibility testing, 118
HIV (Human Immunodeficiency Virus), 79, 79–85, 141–146, *142*
hives, 99
homeostasis, 25, 71
Hong Kong flu, 122
hormones, 46–49, 116–117
house dust, 92, 93, 95, 101
HPA (hypothalamus, pituitary, adrenal) axis, 46–48
human beta-defensin 2 (HBD-2), 73
humor, 61
humoral immunity, 32, 33
hydrochloric acid, 17
hypochondria, 99
hypothalamus, 46, 47, 71

immunity, defined, 13
immunization, 128, 131
immunoglobulin A (IgA), 31, 51, 61
immunoglobulin D (IgD), 31
immunoglobulin E (IgE), 31, 51, 63, 92, 93, 96, 102, 105
immunoglobulin G (IgG), 31, 50, 113, 116, 131
immunoglobulin M (IgM), 31, 39, 116
immunoglobulins (*see* antibodies)
immunotherapy, 102–103

skin, 15, *16*, 149
skin allergies, 93
skin cancer, 54
SLE (systemic lupus erythematosus), 108–110, 117
sleep, 56, 60
smallpox, 138–140
spleen, 17, *18*, 19, 20, 39, 149
Staphyloccus aureus bacteria, 27
stem cells, 150
stomach acid, *16*, 17, 149
Streptoccus bacteria, *67*, 67, 77
stress, 47–49, 99
subunit vaccines, 128
suppressor T cells, 19, 25, 109, 150
sweat, *16*, 17, 149
synovium, 110

tapeworms, *68*, 69

T cells, 11, 15, *21*, 24, 33–37, 54, *56*, 57, *59*, 70, 79, 81–85, 136–137
   types of, 19–20
tears, *16*, 17, 31, 149
TGFb (transforming growth factor), 115
thymidine kinase, 84
thymus gland, *18*, 19, 37, 56, 149
thyroid gland, 71, 107
thyroxine, 71
tissue typing, 118
tonsils, *18*, 149
toxins, 27, 37
toxoids, 126, 132
transformation, 77
transplants, 115–117, *118*, 120–123
trimethoprim, 73
TSH (thyroid stimulating hormone), 71
tuberculosis (TB), 55, 86

tumor necrosis factors, 31, 32, 39
typhoid, *52–53*

ulcers, 70

vaccines, 66, 100, 115, 124–146
vacuoles, 40
varicella, 132, *132*
viral pneumonia, 74
viruses, 10, 13, 26–28, 33, 35–37, 40, 41, 67–85, 89–91 (*see also* specific viruses)
vitamins, 58, 59

Wegener granulomatosis, 108

xenograft, 120
xenotransplants, 120–121

yeast infections, 68